The Countryman

Spring 1994

Volume 99, No. 2

Contents

Articles

Regular features

Poems

Illustrations

Cover: *Spring touches Turville in the Chilterns*
Photograph by Paul Felix

EDITORIAL OFFICE: The Countryman, Sheep Street, Burford, Oxon. OX18 4LH. *Tel: Burford (0993) 822258.*

The Countryman is published six times a year and is on sale by the third Friday of January, March, May, July, September and November.

CONTRIBUTIONS are welcomed, but unaccepted material will be acknowledged only if accompanied by a stamped addressed envelope (or overseas international postage coupons). Manuscripts should be typed, double line-spaced.

SUBSCRIPTION DEPARTMENT (also back numbers, changes of address, etc.): The Countryman, 120–126 Lavender Avenue, Mitcham, Surrey CR4 3HP. *Subscription hot line: 081-646 6672.*

A year's postal subscription in the UK is £12.00; to elsewhere £14.00. A gift subscription to someone else is £1 less. From overseas it costs US \$38 (airmail), US \$25 (surface) or the equivalent in your currency.

ADVERTISEMENTS: The Countryman, Sheep Street, Burford, Oxon. OX18 4LH. *Fax: (0993) 822703.* **Display,** *Tel: Burford (0993) 823602.* **Classified,** *Tel: Burford (0993) 822000/ 823664.*

PUBLISHER: *The Countryman* is published by Link House Magazines Ltd., Link House, Dingwall Avenue, Croydon CR9 2TA. **DISTRIBUTED** by United Magazine Distribution Ltd., Castle House, 37–45 Paul Street, London EC2A 4PB. *Tel: 071-490 2020.*

PRINTED in Great Britain for The Countryman Ltd., by Richard Clay Ltd., Bungay, Suffolk. Typesetting by Express Typesetters Ltd., 11 Riverside Park, Farnham, Surrey GU9 7UG. ISSN 0011-0272.

un A United Newspapers publication

4 US Mailing Agent: Mercury Airfreight International Ltd, 2323 Randolph Avenue, Avenel, NJ 07001. Second class postage paid at Rahway, NJ. USPS 662130.

Outside World

MARKETING

Britain's Countryside on Video!

All prices include VAT but please add 95p towards the cost of postage and packaging PER TAPE.

Title	Price
Land of The Lakes – The Opening Up of Lakeland	£10.99
Land of The Lakes – The Place	£10.99
Lakeland	£10.99
Lakeland's Herries Country	£12.99
The Lake District – A Bird's Eye View	£9.99
Wordsworth's Lake District	£12.99
Discovering the Derbyshire Dales	£10.99
Peak District Panorama	£9.99
Border Heritage	£10.99
Scotland – Land of Contrasts	£10.99
Scotland – Land of Legends	£12.99
James Herriot's Yorkshire *(NEW! Recommended Highly!)*	£12.99
Yorkshire Glory	£10.99
A River's View of Swaledale	£12.99
The Yorkshire Dales of England	£12.99

To order any of these beautiful videos, simply write to us at the address below enclosing . . .
Your name and address
Your payment including postage and packing fee
The titles you require
Daytime telephone number if possible.

**Unit 7, Borough Road.,
Gallowfields Trading Estate,
Richmond, N. Yorks DL10 4ST
Tel/Fax: 0748 826075**

We will despatch your videos as soon as possible, but please allow a maximum of 21 days for delivery in case of stock shortage!

Clip and send this ad for FREE p&p on all orders

GLIDE UPSTAIRS ON A STANNAH STAIRLIFT.

Hello, Stan here. A Stannah Stairlift really can make climbing stairs easy again. For your free information pack, complete and return the coupon or call us today.

When your thoughts turn to stairs turn to Stannah.

☎ **Phone FREE (0800) 715121 or return the coupon below.**

Please complete and return to: Stannah Stairlifts Limited, Dept 7110, FREEPOST, Andover, Hants SP10 3BR.

Are you enquiring for your Household ☐
A relative living elsewhere ☐

Name _____

Address _____

_____

_____

Postcode _____

Tel _____

Stannah
Stairlifts

7

The Countryman

Volume 99, No. 2   Spring 1994

Sheep Street in Spring, by Anne Roper

EDITED BY CHRISTOPHER HALL AT BURFORD, OXFORDSHIRE

Cock-up in Ombersley

☐ Hereford & Worcester County Council has, over the last ten years or so, spent at least £40,000 promoting a scheme to rationalise the public paths of Ombersley, near Droitwich, and six neighbouring parishes. Having pushed the scheme, against fierce opposition, all the way to a public inquiry in mid-January, the county council has now decided it wants to pull out, after wasting its charge-payers' money and the time, costs and efforts of scores of other people who have been involved in preparing or opposing the scheme.

Ombersley seems an unlikely setting for a cock-up of such monumental proportions and the creation of deep ill will between ramblers, the county and parish councils and the local farmers and landowners. Pevsner says in his patronising mode that it is 'a specially rewarding village'. The centre is decked with black-and-white timber-framed houses, pleasing pubs; Ombersley Court, the big house, was built in the early eighteenth century for the first Lord Sandys, and the seventh of that title lives there to this day. The church dates from about a century later and is in the grounds of the court. The surrounding countryside is undistinguished but just what one expects of the English midlands. It rolls very gently. There is an occasional enchanting stream, an occasional low summit with unexpectedly wide views, and everywhere a pinkish sandstone tilth.

It all began in 1982 when a few people on the Ombersley parish council sought to alter the route of a handful of local rights of way. The county is especially rich in public paths but, at Ombersley as elsewhere, the enjoyment of those rights too often depends on the convenience of farmers and owners. Moreover, the county council, which is supposed by law to see that the paths are open for use, was manifestly failing to do so. The solution seemed to be to change the routes of the paths to meet the farmers' convenience. Then there would be no excuse for blocking them and the good people of Ombersley would be able to walk happily ever after.

The scheme snowballed. Owners and tenants saw it as a golden chance to 'lose' the paths they didn't like across fields, and to get walkers away from farmyards for instance. Gradually there emerged a path rationalisation scheme on a huge scale, but propelled by all the same motives which drive the usual small-scale schemes. The farmland managers wanted it because *they* would decide where the public rights should be exercised. A lot of the walking public was apathetic because *they* accept deferentially the paths given them, instead of seeing paths as precious, imperilled rights to be defended; the county council staff picked up the scheme and ran with it, because *they* saw a way out of the endless complaints about path obstructions on which, as highway authority, it is supposed to take action. Appeasement of farmers and landowners was the unspoken watchword in county hall.

Eventually the scheme involved 100 separate public paths totalling some 30 miles in length. Farmers paid up significant sums via the parish council to help the scheme along. As a result many of them professed to believe the changes had already been realised, though nothing of the sort was the case.

The Countryside Commission was persuaded to stump up £16,000 towards the cost of an official at county hall to run the project. The commission thought that the whole thing might prove an interesting experiment — there would be other Ombersleys. All the selfish crew who mutter outworn clichés about updating the paths, modernising the network and fostering good will between farmers and public, began to twitch in hope of a big breakthrough. At last the ancient ways could be made anew in the distorted shape required by the modern farmer, his crops, his diversifications and his security.

The credit for stopping this juggernaut belongs essentially to one man, Edgar Powell, who lives in nearby Worcester, walks the paths of the district and was, at the crucial time, chairman of the county branch of the Ramblers' Association; he saw very early on that the public, the walking public, was going to lose out. True, some farmers might leave paths unobstructed when shifted to routes they approved, but it seemed unlikely that there would be a mass conversion to legality of all these persistent and deliberate path-blockers. True, some pleasant new routes would be created, but even more pleasant existing ones would vanish.

Edgar Powell's doubts about the future behaviour of the farmers were strengthened as the scheme developed. The Ramblers and their ally, the Open Spaces Society, made it clear that they would not consider agreeing to any changes unless the existing paths were cleared of problems and open for untroubled public use. The county's special project officer spent several vain years trying to secure this. Even when chasing the holy grail of rationalisation the farmers and landowners could not kick their addiction to path obstruction.

It became clear that the county council intended to press on with the scheme, but in a way

Do you remember this sad little fellow? He appeared on p.142 of our Winter issue. Just to make him sadder than he seemed anyway, our normally reliable printers managed to mask the caption I had written for him, so that he stood forlorn and unexplained on the page. I shan't try using the caption again. Instead readers are invited to write their own — in not more than 20 words, please. There will be a small prize (£10 in notes) for the reader's caption I consider the best. My judgement is final and entries for the competition should reach **The Countryman,** *Sheep Street, Burford, Oxon* ox18 4lh *by 18 April. Photograph by John Saunders.*

11

which was ultimately the council's undoing.

Most farmland path changes are made by 'diverting' paths. You take one or two paths at a time and alter their routes. It isn't a satisfactory procedure because the criteria for such changes are heavily loaded in favour of owners or tenants and against path-users. Circuitous, unnatural and less pleasant routes result, but at least a path from A to B is preserved.

But the Ombersley scheme had grown beyond that. Farmers and landowners were bartering with the parish and county council; they offered to close a path on one side of the farm in exchange for a new one on the other, or perhaps in the next parish. It was no longer possible to squeeze the changes into the framework of the law providing for *individual* path diversions. The county decided to carry the project through by making two separate path orders, one which would create all the new paths and one which would close existing ones. Between the individual elements of the two sets of proposals direct comparison would rarely be possible.

This is where the scheme hit trouble. The county council knew from a minor case involving just two paths in the parish of Pensax, only a few miles from Ombersley, that it was very doubtful legally if two such orders could be confirmed concurrently. But it foolishly went ahead — and so we arrived at the public inquiry on 18 January.

In form it was the normal inquiry held by the Secretary of State for the Environment whenever a public-path order is opposed. In practice it was much more. There were over 50 people there. The Ramblers had sent their solicitor and their deputy director. The county was represented by a senior solicitor. The inspector was not even going to make the decision himself. The Environment Secretary had 'recovered jurisdiction' and would decide the issue after considering the inspector's recommendation. A national precedent for good or ill was in the making.

The inspector, Mr Brian Evans, whose charm equals his patience, began by setting out an elaborate timetable. He was going to split the orders into 24 groups of paths, each with its allocation of inquiry time. The inquiry would probably last into April. In fact it was adjourned on the opening day.

The crux was the submission by Jerry Pearlman, the Ramblers' solicitor, that the two orders must in law be taken separately, the creation first. Only after that should the inquiry turn to the proposed closures.

Alan Moore for the county council resisted this, for he well knew what it would mean. Creation orders are made when there is public benefit arising from the new path. Almost any new path is going to produce such a benefit, so most if not all would go through. Extinguishments are only accepted when the path is not needed for public use. Quite

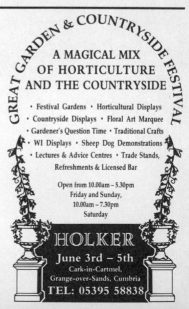

MEPHISTO®

WATERPROOF SHOES THAT BREATHE!

SLACKER
Model DUTCH BOY

SLACKER
Model SLIM JIM

WALKING IS LIVING

14

a few of them might well not get past the inspector. As a result some, perhaps many, of the Ombersley and district farmers would find themselves with *new* paths on their land and — still — some of the old ones they planned to lose. The bartered bargain at the heart of the scheme would be broken. County councillors would face a lot of angry farmers.

Mr Moore asked for a ruling that the orders could be confirmed in the form made. Mr Evans adjourned for a longer than usual tea-break. He came back and refused the county council's request; the Secretary of State was not going to make a legal ruling before the evidence had been heard, but Mr Evans would adjourn the inquiry until 11 March so that the county council could take its own legal advice (something the Countryside Commission had advised it to do several years before).

Less than three weeks later and without waiting for the inquiry to resume, the county council announced that it wished to withdraw the orders. The reasons given were that the Secretary of State and the inspector both refused to be bound by any independent legal advice the council might obtain. There was therefore no guarantee that the minister would feel he had the power to confirm the orders. The council was not prepared to 'commit scarce resources to the project' in these uncertain circumstances, although it had been pouring resources into it for the best part of a decade.

These pages are written before

Village Newsletter

COMPETITION

The Countryman is running its village newsletter competition again this year in association with Action with Rural Communities in England (ACRE). Once again John Timpson, the broadcaster and writer, himself an enthusiastic Norfolk villager, will lead the panel of judges. We hope, as usual, to have a pleasant party here in Burford for the presentation of the awards.

First prize will be a £200 cheque, with £50 each for the runners-up. Winners and runners-up all get a handsome certificate to frame and display in the village hall.

As always we look for newsletters which are lively and which cover the whole community.

Entry forms are now available from *The Countryman*, Sheep Street, Burford, Oxon OX18 4LH. Please send an envelope (at least DL size, i.e. 220 × 110mm) stamped and addressed; mark it NEWSLETTER. Closing date is 26 May. Good luck! — *Editor*.

16

the date of the inquiry's resumption, and nothing is yet certain. It is conceivable that having made its orders, Hereford & Worcester County Council will find it has no power to withdraw them; on the other hand, if it then presents no evidence it seems impossible that the inspector should be able to do anything but refuse them. In other words it does look as if, after much strife and hard work, the Ombersley scheme is dead.

We rejoice because the overweening county council has been humbled, although we recognise that most councillors had little understanding of what was going on. A project presented as something the parish councils wanted, backed by farmers and landowners, blessed by the words 'modernisation' and 'rationalisation', and said to lead to less hassle over the paths in future, understandably won the support of most of the elected members who encountered it and who knew little of paths. But again Edgar Powell and a handful of rambler colleagues get applause for an untiring campaign to awake — in the end successfully — councillors to the inbuilt arrogance and impracticality of the project.

We rejoice because Ombersley will, we hope, be a lesson to other councils contemplating similar exercises. To name one, Bedfordshire is considering just such a scheme in the parishes of Toddington and Chalgrave on the edge of the Chilterns north of Dunstable. It has all the ingredients of another Ombersley — a few promoters working with the parish councils but outside the established path-user organisations, farmers and landowners greedy for change and council officers who put a peculiar concept of efficiency before people.

The law about public paths was never meant to enable wholesale parish-wide (or parishes-wide) changes to be made. Country paths are essentially the organic growths of centuries and must be dealt with as such. Mostly they are just fine where they are and where they have been for a long time. If paths must be changed, let it be done sensitively, by agreement and in the public not the private interest.

□ It so happens that, a couple of weeks after Hereford & Worcester's climb-down, I was personally involved in a battle over footpaths, though a far lesser affair than the Ombersley nonsense.

I was asked by the Oxfordshire Ramblers to represent them at the public inquiry considering the dualling of a stretch of the A43 running north-eastwards from the M40 towards Brackley across the county boundary in Northamptonshire. Half a dozen or so paths are affected by the route and the problem — as always with these schemes — is to ensure that the new road does not smash the network apart. So there were half a dozen places where I had to go and look at the route of the road with plans in my hand and see what the Department of Transport's engineers were proposing for the foot-

18

SHAUGH CHURCH FROM THE STONES OF THE GREAT CIRCLE, SHAUGH MOOR

When I was researching material for our exploration of Dartmoor and South Devon (which begins on p.135), I came across this drawing. It appeared on the front of a combative leaflet issued by the Dartmoor Preservation Association in 1976, when the DPA was struggling to prevent this neolithic stone circle being buried under the waste products of china-clay digging. For the sequel see p.145. But the point is that the drawing was made by Sylvia Sayer, who not only chaired and led that very effective pressure group but could turn her hand to a telling drawing as well as to cogent words — a person of talent indeed.

path or bridle-way crossing the road.

As I approached the north end of the scheme I realised I was treading in hallowed footsteps. I came to a signpost labelled Cottisford and a half mile or so further on one labelled Juniper. Now 'Juniper' is what the devisers of Oxfordshire's signs call Juniper Hill and Juniper Hill is what Flora Thompson called Lark Rise, the tiny, impoverished hamlet in which her heroine Laura (in truth herself) was brought up in the 1880s and '90s

and whose recollections, published some 40 years later, constitute a classic of the British countryside — beautifully written, but also an utterly convincing account of its time, place and people.

This then was the spot on the main road to Oxford to which Flora/Laura's mother used to walk with her baby brother in the prized black wickerwork baby carriage, like an old-fashioned Bath chair on three wheels, with Laura running and skipping beside. And here is how they found

that road —

Although it was a main road, there was scarcely any traffic, for the market town lay in the opposite direction along it, the next village was five miles on, and with Oxford [19 miles away] there was no road communication from that distant point in those days of horse-drawn vehicles. Today [1939], past that same spot, a first-class, tar-sprayed road, thronged with motor traffic, runs between low, closely trimmed hedges. Last year a girl of eighteen was knocked down and killed by a passing car at that very turning. At that time it was deserted for hours together. Three miles away trains roared over a viaduct, carrying those who would, had they lived a few years before or later, have used the turnpike. People were saying that far too much money was being spent on keeping such roads in repair, for their day was over; they were only needed now for people going from village to village.

Now Laura's empty road, Flora's busy tar-sprayed road, is being more than doubled in traffic capacity to feed more vehicles into the M40 striding across the midlands.

As far as footpath and bridle-way users are concerned the M40 was the main problem, for the Department of Transport was refusing to provide a path free of traffic at the massive interchange where the A43 and M40 join. The village of Ardley lies to the west of the motorway and a service area is being built to the east. The department and the Ardley parish council are united in opposing a route for path-users because it might enable nasty people from the service area to reach the village half a mile away.

IN OUR GARDEN

So the department's parsimony and the parish's paranoia are joined to destroy another bit of a path network enjoyed by folk for centuries.

☐ The crocuses and the snow-drops are putting on their annual *sursum corda* display in the garden here at Burford as I write. By the time you read this the daffodils should be trumpeting about the staddle-stones and the old walnut-tree on the bank above the croquet-lawn. Perhaps you will come to see us this spring; I hope so, *The Countryman* garden is always open (no charge) to *Countryman* readers.

But there will be a few days this summer — as usual — when, if you happen to visit, you will be asked to pay a modest fee as you come under the arch of our old coaching-inn and so up the steps to the garden behind. These are the days when I hand the garden over to a local good cause and they use it to make a bit of money.

The Friends of Chipping Norton Theatre (a gallant enterprise operating in a former Salvation Army hall) will be here on the afternoon of 5 June, and a month later (9 July) the Friends of Burford Hospital take their turn. The hospital is a cottage hospital, just 500 yards along Sheep Street from our front door and much valued by the community.

We are also hoping to have the Red Cross one day later in the summer.

Do come!

Christopher Hall

The bright weeping

Nothing as shining today
As the new willow-branches
Against a coal spring sky.

Tomorrow their hairline will
Have aged to a still fawn-green
So swift this season's maturity.

For months I have watched
The tree's ribcage harnessed
In ruthless winter winds,

Droop almost breathless
Under a snow shawl,
Struck dumb with frost.

But the bright weeping begins
With the first young leaf,
The March glimmer of gold.

Photograph by George Hall　　　　　*Poem by Lotte Kramer*

Throwing a bowl

Photographs by
Colin Church

Many hours of careful work go into the making of a handsome bowl in a village pottery.

June Mullarkey makes beautiful bowls, dishes and vases at the Dersing-ham Pottery, near Sandringham in Norfolk. A lump of raw clay is kneaded well, then thrown on a wheel and raised by skilled hands to the shape and thickness suited to its size. ▷▷

After its first
firing, the bowl
is coated with a
'slip' of liquid
glaze (left).
Decoration is
worked into the
still-wet surface
(above) before
the bowl goes
back into the
kiln for its

final firing
(above), which
brings out
the true colour
and surface of
the finished work.
June Mullarkey
sets out her new
wares (right) in
the window of the
village pottery
at Dersingham.   □

CHRIS WATSON

Pegging out and picking holes

Merrills — or nine men's morris — is a once popular board game that is staging a revival in North Yorkshire. People come to watch from as far away as New Zealand, but the winners tend to be locals.

Photographs by the author

IN THE BACK ROOM of the museum, an owl looks down on the players. All is motionless. True, the owl has glass eyes and is stuffed, but the players are real enough. Contemplating their next move, they sit like opposing statues of Rodin's thinker — but for the tweed jacket and anorak and the gingham tablecloth on which the board sits between them.

A player unbends his arm a fraction as if to make a move, hesitates and returns it to his forehead to collect further thoughts. He has a decision to make and it is not an easy one. The hand comes down and starts to tap a peg onto the table in an absent-minded way.

The spectators, no more than a handful of enthusiasts, pay careful attention, but after ten minutes of inactivity they start to chat. A photographer from a national paper studies the players. He bends and peers, clicks and circles and one, without losing his absorption, unfolds a cap from his pocket and puts it on. After five minutes the photographer leaves and the cap is removed. A little further thought and there is a flurry of activity. A peg changes position and then follows a rapid succession of moves until the end of the game, which comes so quietly that it passes almost unnoticed by the audience.

The game is Merrills, a game variously spelt and with many other names, the best-known of which is nine men's morris, and these are the world championships taking place at the Ryedale Folk Museum in the North Yorkshire village of Hutton-le-Hole.

Having gathered a number of old boards into its collection, the museum introduced the merrills championship in 1987 and in 1988 it was expanded to become the world championships. Since then it has been an annual event.

Last year there were three sections to the competition — novices, juniors and the championships themselves. There were players from as far afield as New Zealand and Leominster. 'Well,' said an organiser unabashed but relieved about the visitors from New Zealand, 'it is difficult to attract people from abroad to a village with no public transport.'

Merrills is a board-game with the simplest of rules, easy to learn, and with lots of strategic moves to make it

Merrills has been said to combine the simplicity of noughts and crosses with the strategy of chess. It certainly gives the players pause for thought in the world championships at Hutton-le-Hole.

interesting. The board, with three concentric squares joined along the middle of each side, has 24 holes and each player starts with nine pegs. The aim is to take the opponent's pegs.

The first stage of the game is 'pegging out'. To a champion this stage is as vital to success as the opening moves of a chess game. The players start with a blank board and alternately put pegs onto it. If a player manages to place three pegs in a row — a mill — he can take one of his opponent's pieces, but any pegs in a mill are protected. When all the pegs have been placed on the board, the game moves on to stage two.

Now each player can only move a piece along one of the lines on the board into an empty hole next to it, all the time hoping to make mills and take pieces while protecting his own pegs. It's at this stage that the champions fall comatose. Only their brains are active as the merits of each move are weighed.

When a player has only three pegs left, he moves into stage three of the game. At this point the player can 'fly' round the board, moving pegs to any empty hole.

Merrills was once more widely played. The board can be easily scratched onto the ground and all manner of objects used as pegs.

In a disused railway linesmen's hut in Yorkshire, the author found these old game 'boards' carved on a bench. The nearer one is for fox and geese (similar to solitaire) and the other for merrills.

The Merrills world championships were held last September in the Ryedale Folk Museum at Hutton-le-Hole, North Yorkshire.

Farm-workers would mark out boards on corn-bin lids and I have seen a board carved into the bench of a railway linesmen's hut. Boards chiselled in stones are to be found in many abbeys and were probably used by the builders. Others are found carved into the wood of choir-stalls in churches and cathedrals — and Henry VIII's sailors must have played the game because a board cut into the top of a barrel was found on the warship *Mary Rose*, raised in 1982 after 437 years under the waters of the Solent.

Outdoor boards were at one time popular and both John Clare and Shakespeare referred to them. Titania, in *A Midsummer Night's Dream*, berates Oberon for his effect on the weather —

> The fold stands empty in the drowned field,
> And crows are fatted with the murrion flock,
> The nine men's morris is fill'd up with mud;
> And the quaint mazes in the wanton green,
> For lack of tread are undistinguishable: . . .

Here, at the Ryedale museum, the problem of the sodden outdoor board has been solved by using a large plastic sheet, and visitors stand on the damp grass, puzzling their next move. Children rush between the two-foot-high pieces and vital strategies are thwarted as the youngsters topple the pegs and replace them haphazardly.

The last of the indoor matches is late on Sunday afternoon. The spectators are quiet and watchful. It is not an easy sport. The boards are no more than a foot square and the position of the pegs is difficult to see.

A player moves and whistles tunelessly through his teeth. The table creaks with the tension. There is long thought. 'Oooh,' his opponent leans back on his chair, eyes closed. 'Ah, mmm.' The monosyllables each have a different meaning — surprise, admiration, questioning. He thinks some more and the two players start to talk about the game. Their speech is incomprehensible, but in a world championship that is not a surprise. On the other hand, the two players are both from North Yorkshire. There is, it seems, a difficult choice between moves and the problem of being 'limited to yan'. The move is made and they fall quiet again. The referee in the corner eats her sandwiches. Tomato in hand, she walks over to try to hurry them up.

There are no flags falling, no tantrums, no accusations — and when, at the end of the day, the first and second in the world championships come from a dale a mere stone's throw from the museum, it only goes to show what a small world it is. ☐

32

The *Countryman*

comes from the country

A postal subscription will bring it direct to your door six times a year . . .

This is where we make **The Countryman** — in a one-time coaching-inn (above) on quiet Sheep Street in the little Cotswold town of Burford. There is a long and lovely garden behind (which readers are always welcome to visit) and a stunning view over the Windrush valley to the hills beyond.

This is why **The Countryman** always gives you a true country flavour — the country is where it comes from. It is written and illustrated by country people who tell of people and places, crafts and customs, wildlife and waysides that they know and love.

To savour that flavour six times a year has never been easier. A subscription now (all post and packing costs are included, of course) is *only* £12 a year — no more than it costs to buy the same six issues over the counter.

For yourself, for your friends and relatives, near or far, **The Countryman** is a sure passport to the incomparable British countryside. There is a subscription form just over the page . . . ▷▷

34

THELMA K. SYKES

Daring dabchicks

Drawings by the author

A little grebe sails out to repel intruders.

IT WAS SPRING. Yet as foul a day as the Highlands can beget — that day I first found the loch. The water surface was rain-beaten silver. A mallard with her brood sought shelter against a log, part-submerged in a peaty pool. The ducklings huddled in her lee, but the weight of the rain's bombardment bobbed them perilously in the water, and they had difficulty in keeping at her side.

The shore of the loch was indented with many secluded bays, and this bay was dominated by two pines which had crashed into the water. Wind-whipped waves threw spindrift creaming against their entangled roots. Splendidly tall they had been, now skeletons toppled in the loch, with contorted limbs and only memories of ancient Caledon. I watched ripples encircle each raindrop, spreading ribbons of Celtic pattern. The loch seemed not of my time.

Suddenly the pattern broke. From the centre of the turbulence surged a little grebe. Water glazed his head, gathered in droplets and was shrugged away with his next dive. Heedless of the rain he went, diving and surfacing so buoyantly that he seemed momentarily to clear the water. He was in his element. And, as we shared the storm in that lonely place, I too began to feel comfortably warm.

▷▷

If the great crested grebe is the ballerina of the water-bird world (see p. 28 of our last issue), then the little grebe is surely the diva. It is not that the great crested has no voice — it is just that the barking, growling, croaking, twanging, clicking and mooing with which the larger grebe communicates is as nothing to the vibrato of a little grebe. If you hear a vivacious trilling deep within the cover of a stand of reeds, then a little grebe is singing. And if the trills play up and down the scale to reach a crescendo, that's a dabchick pair duetting.

It's not surprising that the little grebe (or dabchick) should be the most vocal of all our grebes. It is, after all, the only one not to carry coloured head ornaments during the breeding season. Such finery would be of little use to a bird which spends so much time in dense cover. The song is a better advertisement.

And, in all other respects, the little grebe comes as well equipped for its water-borne life as its larger relatives. It shares with them the thick insulating plumage. It has the same multi-purpose legs and feet set at the back of the body. Like them, it can change its specific gravity, so that it can submerge without diving. All the grebes can do it, but the little grebe has this manœuvre down to a fine art.

Approach any lake, gravel-pit or loch, and note the characteristic dumpy shape of a little grebe some way in the distance. No matter how stealthily you approach, you will have been observed. The dabchick allows you to come just so close to the shore, and then it disappears. Sometimes I have watched the bird dive well out on the open water; then waited and waited in vain for it to resurface. What happens to all of these little grebes that sink without trace?

I've spent countless days at the loch since that first encounter with the little grebe. Sometimes the water is busy with tufted duck, other days pass quietly with a secretive pair of widgeon. The silver birches might ring

A pair of exotic Slavonian grebes, the object of a male dabchick's aggression.

with the mixed voices of titmice and treecreepers; there are siskin days, and days of silence.

Sometimes ill weather re-creates the choppy waves of that first visit, but there are soft days too, with warm thermals for soaring buzzards, the loch not water, but mirrored glass. The half-submerged pines are settled lower now, root and reflection sculpted together.

Now it is spring again, and the loch reverberates to the trilling song of the grebe. The drowned pines, sea-changed, secretly keep this year's nest, built on a raft of vegetation trapped by their upflung roots. The routines are familiar: her vigil on the nest; her mate diving out on the loch; gentle greetings as the pair change over the care of the eggs — just as in years before. Sandpiper and nesting golden-eye go about their ways. The sun sets on continuity and order, but is to rise the next day upon confusion.

The male grebe forages well out in the loch. Suddenly his pace changes and he is paddling strongly towards another bird. My binoculars focus sharply on the golden horns and brilliant carmine eye of a Slavonian grebe. Almost at once a second Slavonian surfaces close by. The pair moves slowly forward, side by side, heads dipping in gestures of ritualised preening.

To the artist-naturalist these birds are a rare and wonderful sight; to the little grebe they are intruders. He storms closer, thrusting feet power him into pattering flight. Startled, the Slavonians skitter over the water until airborne, then veer out of ken in hunchbacked flight. The little grebe subsides with a splash, shakes himself, and turns for home.

Confidingly, though, the Slavonians stay on. The loch is large with many secluded bays, and suits them well. But they move out into mid-loch for fishing, where day after day the antagonism continues. The little grebe is the aggressor. He has time for his family only when the larger grebes are lost to view. As soon as they drift into the open he launches his attack, hurtling low over the water, all feet and splash and anger.

He has subterfuge, too. Sometimes his speed subsides as he nears his rivals. Slowly he submerges, head and neck only above the water, a watching periscope. Then, without a ripple, he disappears, seconds later to burst through the water-surface beneath the very flanks of the trespassers. Panic! The Slavonian grebes are startled into flight.

My most recent visit to the loch was as wet and cold as the first one, but then it was November and so to be expected. The storm clouds gave an evening's dusk at mid-day and the view over the water was blurred and grey. But there, out on the loch, a dabchick dived, heedless of the dark.

I remembered the glint of the sun on those gold-maned Slavonians. Did they stay out the season? Were there young Slavonians on the loch this year? Whatever the answer, they will have deserted the loch now for the coast, and will spend their winter at sea. The little grebe stays on. Just for now he has full possession of the waters which he scarcely ripples as he sinks from view — and bobs to the surface with proud buoyancy. □

Selling out

A gentle rain starts to fall
as I look out over the pasture,
over land no longer mine. Silver droplets
form a pattern on the upturned leaves of trees I planted.

This is the last of it.
Of springs I've spent watching life
take root here again and again,
spiralling down into the rich earth.

Like trees tossed by the storm, our dreams
rose and fell here, rotten leaves scattered
at our feet that provided fertile ground
for still more dreams.

Tracing the first steps I took here
over rocks and grass, I stand
on the flimsy bridge we built across the creek
remembering how good it was to own a piece of all that was.

Not much to move or haul away now,
just a few odd possessions tossed helter-skelter in the
barn where dust settles quietly
over the lost days of our lives.

Deborah Robinson

ELIZABETH SEAGER

From an Evenlode garden

Grey thoughts
in a green shade

Drawing by Brian Walker

EVERY GARDEN has its unique *genius loci*, the presiding
genius or spirit of the place. Much thought was given
to this by eighteenth-century garden-designers, who
attempted to capture the elusive underlying mood, and
to emphasise it with carefully chosen planting and
statuary.

The spirit of my own garden is an informal one, as
befits the position of our cottage on the edge of open
fields and woods. Its boundary walls are the natural
stone of the landscape — golden-grey Cotswold limestone — and the garden artefacts, seats, pots, trellis, bird
tables, are of wood, clay or stone.

In keeping with the age of the small cottage, which
probably dates from the late seventeenth century, the
garden plants are mostly traditional, though not entirely
authentic. I grow the flowers that cottagers have loved
since Elizabethan times — Jack-in-the-green primroses
and rose plantain with its odd rosettes in place of the
usual slender poker-heads. Columbines, Jacob's ladder,
sweet rocket and feverfew jostle together, with Victorian
and Edwardian introductions such as regal lilies, for-
sythia and fragrant viburnum.

Ancient and modern roses scent the air — 'Old Blush
China' and 'Rosa Mundi', the 1920s' beauty 'Souvenir
de Claudius Denoyel', and 'The Countryman' rose, one
of David Austin's recent English roses, bred to combine

the beauty of old-fashioned varieties with the vigour of modern hybrids.

This informal, slightly untidy mixture suits our surroundings, the flowers and foliage flowing round the cottage in a tranquil swirl, merging gently into the countryside in a haze of leaves and a tracery of twigs.

With few exceptions, little of the twentieth century intrudes on the scene. No aerial sprouts from our roof, for we have no television; and no garish plastic whirly sullies the grass plot, for on Mondays I hitch up a removable clothes-line and my washing flaps in front of the outhouse, as in years past.

A 40-year-old electricity pole stands in the back corner of the garden, complete with its ugly cables, but it can be

'An artist might work wonders on these bins, creating a variety of designs suitable for different gardens ...'.

seen only from one aspect, and the pole has an important redeeming feature as a haunt of birds. It provides a perch for tawny owls who sit there quarrelling and hooting at night as they scan the garden for prey; and the pole contains several holes where woodpeckers wedge hazelnuts taken from the bushes below, tapping loudly as they push them in with their fierce beaks. In early autumn, swallows and martins swing and chatter on the wires, as they gather for their long migration.

Apart from one or two modern drainpipes, plastic played little part in the garden scene, until last year when our district council introduced a pilot scheme of new wheeled refuse-bins. Ours arrived at the gate one spring day, not green as expected, but a dark grey, shiny plastic monster, nearly four feet high, described in the official leaflet as 'relatively attractive', but as out of place as it could possibly be in a cottage garden, and a decided insult to our *genius loci*. Worse still, the bin was enlivened with a dazzling red-and-white brand label. Fortunately, this peeled off, and we repositioned it inside the lid.

Various reasons — including ash-disposal and the garden layout — dictate a place near the back door for this horror. Much too large to fit the secluded nook that hid our now redundant dustbins, it stands exposed to the gate, glowering at me implacably every morning like a gloomy monolith, but with none of the mystery or patina of an ancient menhir.

With an enormous effort of imagination it might be viewed in the half-light as a minimalist geometric sculpture — but a particularly nasty one, and quite inappropriate to the surroundings. When it comes to disguising the beast, I own myself defeated, for there is no space for a screen of ivy-covered trellis or bushy evergreen.

I long to give it *trompe-l'oeil* treatment — nothing so vulgar as graffiti you understand, but a cunning transformation that would turn it to a thing of beauty.

An artist might work wonders on these bins, creating a

variety of designs suitable for different gardens — *à la grecque*, with caryatids; maritime, with a ship's figurehead; rustic, with milkmaid, or trellis and ivy; Cotswold, with a pattern of lichened stone; or formal, with a potted topiary design. The variations are endless, and would greatly enliven the dustmen's job too.

However, the council would obviously have little truck with such ambitious ideas, for they won't even allow me to paint the monster green to merge with the garden plants. They fear 'the setting of a precedent which could lead to the more widespread defacement of bins'.

In return, I could argue that the bin defaces my garden in no uncertain way, but somehow I feel that those who impose dark grey wheelies on a rural landscape would have no time for 'a green thought in a green shade' and would care little or nothing for my *genius loci*.   □

Since the above was written, an alternative wheeled bin has become available, much smaller than the original. This is now on test and seems to be more in scale with our needs and surroundings. — *E.S.*

This is the last article in the series 'From an Evenlode garden'.

Moon dial

Waking at owl drift, clock has stopped,
And night is timeless — till wind dries the sky.
Then all the room becomes a dial
Where moonlight marks the hours
On fixed, familiar digits,
Striking two, three, four,
On table, mirror, chair;
Tolling the half hours silently
On dish, jug, chest of drawers —
A silver timepiece running through the dark,
Slowed briefly by a cog of cloud,
Then, finally, by dawn
And chiming birds.

Elizabeth Seager

DAWN ROBERTSON

Last man in the dale…

Photographs by Peter Koronka

James Potter mends a drystone wall in Bretherdale. Once 100 people lived and farmed here but now there are only three.

TODAY, JAMES POTTER is the only farmer left living in Bretherdale, a valley near Shap in Cumbria, where nearly 100 people lived and worked two centuries ago. His story is the story in miniature of what has happened to rural Cumbria in that time, with Bretherdale an extreme instance.

Sheep were at the centre of the old economy, with wool and cottage industries such as stocking-knitting and weaving as the mainstays.

The manor anciently belonged to Bigland Abbey in Yorkshire, but passed to the Wharton and then the Lowther families. It is first recorded in 1247 as Britherdal and its name is Old Norse for 'valley of the brothers'. Proud yeomen and hard-working tenant farmers, each with a few acres of good land in the dale bottom and grazing rights on the fell, generation after generation worked in the same manner, passing on shepherding skills along with the Norse-based dialect, culture and

44

customs of the Cumbrian farmer.

The valley is dotted with derelict farmhouses — reminders of the days of prosperity when confidence in the future of farming led men to invest their energy in miles of drystone walls, improved pastures and field-houses for keeping stock and feed during the northern winters.

They invested in the future of their children too, by providing an education so that those who could not stay to work the farms could move to the cities to earn their livings. A free school was built in Greenholme in 1738 and endowed with £400 by George Gibson for the education of poor children. A few years ago there were no children left, so the school was closed and turned into a community centre; but it turned out there was no community left, so it is now an outdoor education centre.

Over the past two centuries the population has dwindled from its peak of about 100, to 48 by 1884, and now only three people are left living in the valley — James, his wife Christine and their baby daughter, Dawn.

By the time the 1851 census was compiled the heyday of Cumbrian farming was over, with some of the higher fellside farms already abandoned. Thirty years later only nine farms were left, with agricultural depression claiming victims such as Hawse, Daglum and Scalehow, which today are just piles of rubble.

The nine farms continued into the early years of this century, when economics again bit deep into the hill-farming community. Families who had lived in the

Bretherdale Head was once a proud yeoman's home, but it has been empty and derelict for many years, along with many other farmhouses in the dale.

dale for generations, such as the Longmires, Pratts and Watsons, moved away never to return — but the Potters hung on.

Low Stead has belonged to the Potter family for generations and in 1851 was the home of 53-year-old John Potter and his son Thomas, who were farming 71 acres. John's wife, Agnes, ran a grocery business, no doubt to augment the farming income; in Cumbria at least the idea of farm diversification is not new.

James started farming Low Stead (now a 135-acre farm) four years ago and readily admits that it is hard work. For the time being he has had to keep a part-time job at a nearby filling-station to help pay the grocery bill, but he optimistically says that the farm is starting to make a bit of money.

James was born and brought up at Midwath Stead, where his parents farmed. He was the third of six children and, when his father became ill and his mother was crippled with rheumatism, he helped with the farm. His brothers and sister moved out of farming and all now live in the nearby village of Orton.

'I lived in Tebay for five or six years and I always said I wouldn't come back. Before I left I got a job in Tebay because the farm would not have supported two households. I was working shifts, morning or afternoon, at the filling-station and the other half of the day I worked at home,' explained James.

However, when his father died and his uncle retired

James Potter with his wife Christine and their daughter Dawn, plus Ben the sheepdog, outside their lonely Bretherdale home at Low Stead.

Bretherdale is only a mile from the M6 motorway as it climbs over Shap summit, but it is now almost uninhabited. James Potter runs sheep in the valley bottom, just outside the Lake District National Park.

in 1989, something in his bones called him back to Bretherdale. James now keeps Rough Fell sheep and suckler cattle and has three meadows in the bottom of the valley, plus some pastures, woodland and grazing rights on the fell.

Both James and Christine work on the farm and even the baby, Dawn, tries to tackle the sheep along with Ben, the ten-year-old sheepdog, who is blind in one eye and has to be sent round the sheep in a certain direction so that he can see them.

Up on the fell, overlooking the dale idyllic in the sunshine, James thinks of the future: 'There's going to come a time when it's not so much farming as looking after the land. It will be a kind of glorified park-keeping. This has been designated an Environmentally Sensitive Area and I have just signed up to follow the rules of the system. It's going to pay people living in places like this.

'It's more of an incentive to look after the land and to keep fewer animals. That may have been the downfall of a lot of these farms because there were so many sheep that the living made from them became less and less. Headage grants encouraged farmers to keep more, but the value fell. This ESA system encourages farmers to look after the land more and keep far fewer sheep, and in the long term it could help the market.'

The rest of Bretherdale is farmed by John Thwaites from Eskew Beck, who inherited the land from his grandfather who bought several farms as they came up for sale, leaving the houses empty and amalgamating the land to make one viable farm for his family. Mr Thwaites's grandfather was the last person to live at New House in Bretherdale and, when he died 30 years ago, his son locked the door of the house, with all the ancient family furniture within. His father wanted to keep it as a kind of museum to his family, but the temptation was too great for thieves who raided the isolated farmhouse, so it now stands empty and crumbling.

Bretherdale Head was once a fine farmhouse but now its gutters are full of weeds, its windows are broken and there are nettles everywhere. Behind it is an even older house, long since abandoned and green with ferns and mosses.

Two other former farms are now holiday cottages. Another sign of change is the two barns for sale with planning permission to convert into dwellings. Midwath Stead Farm itself is for sale, but it seems unlikely that a buyer will come along who wants to farm the land. Local lads who want to set up in farming just would not have the money.

Older folk who remember how things were may think that James Potter is lucky because he has had the chance to give farming a go in the old way. But, as he struggles and works all the hours of the day and night, perhaps he sometimes wonders if it is worth it. ☐

STEPHEN SAINSBURY

Can we get there by candlelight?

Drawings by Reg Finbow

OUR COTTAGE is set high in the Lowther Hills in south-ern Scotland; deep snow fills the road in front and thick flakes still fall from a dark sky. Through the cottage windows comes the glow of candlelight and a roaring fire: no harsh electric lights, no electric fire, no television.

This is our home today.

Why should two ambitious people want to recreate the lifestyle of the miners who lived in our cottage two or three hundred years ago?

Two years ago, Karen and I were walking a few miles from the cottage, on a small country road, when a heli-copter flew low overhead. We looked up in dismay at the load of steel girders slung beneath it. A few weeks later a line of ugly pylons had sprouted in the place of the fir wood which used to shade the road up into the hills. The trees had been uprooted, the wildlife displaced, just to give the village more of what it already had, electricity.

When we reached home we switched on the lights and began to complain to each other.

'But *we* use electricity,' Karen said, suddenly.

'We could hardly manage without it,' I laughed.

'Couldn't we?' she questioned. 'Are you sure?'

Karen was sure we could do without electricity, but I wasn't. I worried about hot water, the washing, the cook-ing, the computers, the fridge, the lights, the hoovering . . .

It took us a few weeks to decide. I kept bringing up

'They asked us to reconsider our decision. Their public relations man came to see us . . .'.

new problems and Karen had a solution to them all, in theory. We decided to try managing without electricity for a trial period of six months.

We sent a letter to Scottish Power: 'Please cut us off'. Three months later, Scottish Power replied. They asked us to reconsider our decision. We wrote back insisting. Their public relations man came to see us. Again we asked to be cut off. It seemed that had we not paid our bill they would have rushed to do what we wanted, but when we asked to be disconnected they didn't want to know.

But they finally agreed. Two sheepish-looking men with wire-cutters appeared on the first of October, and seemed surprised when we happily invited them in to do the deed. Twenty minutes later we were without electricity.

We had deliberately chosen to come off as the nights were drawing in and the cold was deepening. We live at 1,400ft above sea level so the winters here can be interesting.

Darkness came and I reached for the light switch. Nothing, of course. And stupidly I had waited until dark to prepare the meal — stumbling about with a candle and eventually burning two potatoes in their jackets in the roaring and uncontrollable fire. We had sandwiches! We kept treading on our seven cats, who hadn't noticed the difference. What *had* we done?

We soon found that, like most things in life, coming off electricity had its negative points. The problems I'd raised, and we'd 'solved' when we still had electricity, suddenly had to be faced.

Hot water seemed an easy one, as we had a back-boiler behind the living-room fire which worked wonderfully well. But chopping wood for the fire could be a nightmare first thing in the morning, when we often wake up to frost on the *inside* of the windows and when the temperature is minus ten on the woodshed thermometer; and when the sap in the wood is frozen solid and the axe slides off ineffectively and dangerously. But, fortunately, last winter did not match that of 1947, when snow filled the village square to the rooftops. I soon managed to build up a store of cut wood on the milder days, and learned to prepare the morning's wood the afternoon before.

Washing clothes was never going to be as easy without electricity as with, but our old washing-machine had been so unreliable that we had had plenty of practice. But the drying was a different matter. Our tumble-dryer had been a very efficient, if noisy machine, and without it during the winter the clothes often stayed on the line for days, or even weeks on end, receiving soaking

'They finally agreed. Two sheepish-looking men with wire-cutters appeared and seemed surprised when we happily invited them in to do the deed . . .'.

after soaking from the rain and snow. A clothes-horse has helped enormously.

Cooking was one of my main worries. We cook on the open fire, using a grill borrowed from the old electric oven. Nowadays frying is something I only do when I feel particularly reckless. We have had our share of disasters — the pizzas that burn underneath but are raw on top, and the parsnips we forgot that burned away into tiny, shrivelled matchsticks of baked carbon. But curries are easy, as are hotpots, toast, soup and rice. It's a case of choosing the right sort of meal. Cooking is now far more sociable than it was, and usually a lot quicker.

The computers were a difficulty. We had been running a small mail-order business from home, and had come to rely on them. But then we'd managed for years before without, so we switched back to the old system: a card index for records and a manual typewriter for letters. It was, amazingly, more efficient — and much quieter without the printers running all day.

The fridge passed away peacefully. We do not eat meat, and had both shortly before given up dairy products as well. We switched to a bucket of water in which we stand soya milk, fruit juice and margarine. Of course we miss ice in our drinks and 24-packs of ice lollies, but with snow lying for 50 to 100 days a year, perhaps I'll get round to building an ice house.

We had many options for lighting the house, and we tried them all. First oil-lamps, but they were far too noisy, introducing the sound of an express train into the living-room. Battery lamps were useless in a large room, and I broke our only torch after a few days. We soon found the ideal solution — candles. Now we use nothing else. They are wonderfully relaxing, and cheap, but a little hair-raising when we are trying to rescue a vole or rabbit from one of our cats in the middle of the night. I'm glad no one else can see me running around the bedroom with a candle and a small box for the casualty.

I do miss the vacuum cleaner. We have replaced the carpets with rugs laid on the stone floor. Unfortunately we live on an unmade road, so it is difficult to keep the cottage spotless. But there are compensations; each Sunday I treat myself to a rug-beating session, which is a great way to relieve tension.

Word soon spread around the village. We hadn't been known for our eccentricity beforehand. We had expected a negative reaction, but to our surprise nearly everybody was very supportive. A few even seemed envious. Living in a conservation village, we felt we were really living up to our designation.

We felt good. We no longer felt responsible for the pylons ruining the hillsides, for the power stations or for the pollution they cause. Our original six-months deadline soon passed, almost unnoticed.

And now, more than a year later, the cottage is beginning to look genuinely non-electric. The fittings are starting to vanish under redecoration, and most of our old electric appliances have been sold. A few things have been converted: an extension lead serves as a washing-line and electric wall-mounted candlesticks now hold real candles. The cottage has gained new space, and an elegance that having electricity prevented.

Our lives have changed enormously. We have taken to listening to the radio and Karen is now writing plays for Radio Four. I have found time to take up painting. We both have time to read for degrees, and studying is far easier without the distraction electricity brings. And we have more money in our pockets.

A week or two ago the village suffered one of its regular power cuts — for a whole day — and we didn't even notice. □

Devon's great
rood-screens

Photographs by **George H. Hall**

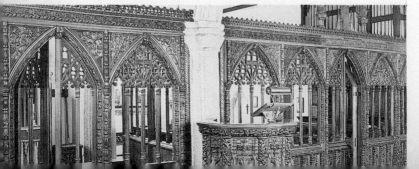

Most churches have a rood-screen separating the nave from the chancel. The earliest screens were simple stonework, but later they blossomed into oaken screens. Devon is especially rich in fine screens, which rise to meet a great beam or bressumer with decorated wainscoting below. These examples are all from Dartmoor and South Devon which we explore on p. 129.

The screen at **Bovey Tracey** (left) with richly-carved fourfold frieze is said to date from 1427. The paintings of apostles and prophets on the wainscoting are from the early sixteenth century. In the church of St. Michael at **Ashton** (below) there are 32 painted figures of saints, while at **Lustleigh** (below left) the corresponding figures are carved statuettes.

▷ ▷

In St. Winifred's church at **Manaton** on Dartmoor (right) there are sixteenth-century paintings of saints in lively colours, their faces gouged out during the Reformation. At **Exminster** (below), between the Exe and the M5, the screen has intricately-carved fan coving and frieze, but at **Ilsington** (far right) the design is more restrained. Here the glory is the wagon roof above the screen. □

JOHN MACLEOD

The dancing daffodils
of a distant isle

Photographs by the author

EASTER VISITORS to the island of North Uist in the
Western Isles of Scotland get a colourful welcome when
their ferry arrives at the harbour of Lochmaddy. Lining
the roads from the harbour are thousands upon thousands of daffodils. It's a magnificent sight, unique in the
sea-swept landscapes of the Outer Hebrides, and it all
began in 1906, when a solicitor named Wilson built a
house here and began creating a garden.

In 1932 the house was bought by Inverness County
Council, to be converted into a residence and surgery
for a new general practitioner under the Highlands and
Islands health scheme. This was my late father (Dr A. J.
Macleod) and he was assisted by my late mother (Dr
Julia). They took over a garden that was quite unusual
for this area. The various solicitors and their wives had
developed a wonderful array of flower-beds, sheltered by
small hedges, on different levels down the slope to the
seashore. The flat paths were formed by slabs of white
marble. My parents were able to keep it fine for some
years, but increasing pressures meant that it gradually
declined.

My wife Lorna and I came in 1973, but we have not
been able to revive it. However, one feature that we have
developed is the wonderful collection of daffodils, of
which there are about 45 varieties — we try to add a new
breed now and then. It is likely that some have survived

Many thousands of daffodils have been planted beside the roads from the harbour at Lochmaddy on the Isle of North Uist, making a dazzling display to greet springtime visitors. This unique tradition has its roots more than 80 years ago, at the house where Dr MacLeod lives.

from the original planting in 1906.

This is despite the heavy salt spray, a period when cattle had access for grazing and (for most of the years) an annual invasion by local sheep which would burst through or jump any fence to get at the only fresh greenery visible in the early part of the year. The soil is thick, acid peat and some varieties seem to have survived and multiplied better than others. On the west coast of North Uist, with soil that has a very high content of shell-sand, there is a farmhouse garden with some 40 varieties of daffodil and it seems to me that different ones thrive there in the soil of contrasting content.

Although my parents inherited many different types, they added some new ones most years and my wife and I have continued the custom. In the late 1930s there was

an early spring run of salmon into the island lochs and one of the intrepid anglers who came to try to catch them was the late Harold Beale, who was then a director of Carters' Seeds. He was surprised and intrigued to see the fine show of blooms at Lochmaddy and, later that year, he sent my parents two large sacks of mixed bulbs. These were eventually planted and now, with multiplication and the intermittent additions, the spring display is so great that we can pick 1,000 and it is scarcely noticed. Although the garden is drenched with salt spray during winter and spring gales, we get very little snow or frost. This leads to early flowering and we usually pick the first bunch at the end of February (once, at the end of January).

The picked flowers soon find their way to the houses of the elderly and to the hospitals and residential homes in Uist and Lewis.

Each year, we try to dig up and separate some of the larger clumps but, by the time they are ready for lifting, the dreaded Hebridean midge is active and, as soon as you disturb the dying leaves, the midges burst out and attack any bare skin.

In 1983 half a mile of new road was built through the

Snow is rare on South Uist, but it does sometimes fall and then the early daffodils take on an extra brilliance. For many years, the residents have been transplanting bulbs to extend the display area.

village and, at the same time, the community council managed to get the village declared effectively 'sheep-free'. I got permission from the roads department and, over three autumns, volunteers helped me to transplant

24,000 bulbs into the soft peat on the sides of the new road. Despite occasional forays from wandering sheep, these have multiplied well and we have continued to plant out more bulbs each autumn since then.

In this windswept and relatively barren island, the first daffodil buds pointing towards the low sun indicate that the gales will be lessening and that soon we should be sharpening the faithful spade, ready to dig the vegetable patch and take the top layer of turf off the peat bank. The daffodils give us great pleasure in the spring — and then many sore backs later in the year when we dig up clumps for transplanting. ☐

March daffodils

With each squeeze of the bulb,
The sepals snap
Open, unoverlap.
The mirror lifts from earth's eye

With an angel-flash in the dark.
Each zoom corona
Makes its time-lapse exposure:
Stills, to authenticate the Spring's puff.

John Greening

INTREEGUING. Common Ground, the charity that encourages people to rejoice in their own familiar patch of the environment, is running Tree-dressing Day again this year. It doesn't happen until the first week of December, but — from the experience of previous events — Common Ground warns that you cannot start planning too soon.

If you want to know more, and especially if you might organise or join in a tree-dressing — *any* tree — there is to be a seminar at the Natural History Museum, Cromwell Road, London on the afternoon of 18 May. The fee is £12 (£6 if unwaged) and you can get details and a booking form from Common Ground, 41 Shelton Street, London WC2H 9HJ.

DOREEN GRIFFIN

Birds in your hands

Engravings by Thomas Bewick

*'The trees with the rookeries . . .
are still there . . .'.*

EVERY SPRING it was the same, the big trees in our garden in Cheshire yielded a crop of discarded baby rooks.

I now realise that you should not try to rear wild animals and birds; it's unnatural. But what do you do when faced by two small children, crying, and holding out a bedraggled bundle of shaggy, wet feathers?

'Please Mum, please!'

You take it reluctantly and mess about with fountain-pen fillers — like the books say, but it doesn't work — and then with a teaspoon handle which does. You give them unnatural food like bread and milk, and put them in cardboard boxes lined with old tights and try to keep them warm. Mostly they die and you are relieved, in spite of pretending to be sorry for the children's sake.

But sometimes they survive and grow and thrive and turn into big rooks with a mother fixation for *you*. At the time my husband John worked with broilers and brought them some pellets. But, whatever the reason, thrive a few of them did.

I think the parents pushed some of the baby rooks from the nest because they were deformed. But one or two must have fallen out through sheer youthful exuberance. We once watched for a whole afternoon while the

63

'The parents usually sat in a tree quite near the house . . . .'.

parents cajoled and coaxed a baby back into the tree — up shrubs, into taller shrubs, into trees and finally back into its own nest — only to see it fall straight out again a minute or so later!

It was one such adventurer that decided I was its mother. I fed it for a few days until I realised that when I wasn't there it was quite happily pecking about, picking up the food I'd let fall from the spoon handle. It was furious when I decided to stop feeding by hand and would knock the bowl of food out of my hand, and stomp up and down the perch in a great rage. I decided it was time to teach it to fly, and I let it sit on my hand, encouraging it to flutter from hand to perch, gradually moving further and further away from the perch. I suppose it would have learnt to fly anyway, but it seemed a good idea at the time.

Eventually it flew about in the garden but seemed only able to fly upwards, so that if it accidentally got onto a low branch, every subsequent flight took it higher and higher until at last it was on the top of the tree and seemed uncapable of working out how to fly down. Once, after three days of being called, answering my calls with loud and ever more desperate squawks, it fell out of the tree and I jumped up and fielded it before it once more flew upwards. It fell asleep on my hand, head tucked under its wing, safely home again.

As it grew bigger, it decided that I was not only mother but also its mate, because whenever it saw me or heard my voice it would ruffle its head and neck feathers so that it seemed to be wearing a ruff and pantaloons. I was told that this was a mating posture, and try as I would to call the rest of the family in time, no one else ever saw this. I think that in the end they didn't believe me.

If anyone was holding a lighted cigarette, it would snatch at the glowing end and push the hot ash under each wing. It would also spread-eagle itself at the sight of a lighted cigarette. This astonished us at the time, and it was years later that I heard this action called 'anting'. It seems that birds pick up ants and tuck them under their wings, although I still don't understand why. Perhaps someone could tell me?*

One night, when John arrived home very late, he was surprised to find two rooks, one magpie and a baby owl in the little lean-to shed at the back of the house. Only one rook had been there when he went to work in the morning.

The owl had fallen down the chimney, which was boarded up and had a gas oven in front of it. Squeaks and strange noises made the children insist that I pull everything out to see what was making the noise. Sitting half-way up the chimney was a ball of pale grey fluff with

---

*The Countryman's natural-history editor, Euan Dunn, says rooks and other species use ants as an insecticide and perhaps an antibiotic (against fungus, for example). In this case the rook was substituting the readily available ash for ants. Anting birds often spread-eagle themselves above the ants.

big blue eyes and long lashes. When we got it down it swivelled its head from side to side, blinking seductively.

'Oh no,' I said, 'you've got to feed them on live mice and bits of fur coat, and I'm *not* doing that.'

I put it on the roof of the shed, hoping that the parents, which usually sat in a tree quite near the house, would come for it. There were wails of protest from the children in the morning when the little owl was still sitting on the roof, very wet and miserable. We brought it in and I tried to feed it some dog-meat. Prising the small, sharp beak open was incredibly difficult until it suddenly shot open from ear to ear, terrifying me. I thought its head had broken off. It finished off the tin of dog-food and flew in a lazy, undulating sort of way round and round the kitchen. The children were entranced.

Luckily, I found someone who didn't mind the live mice and fur-coat routine, and the owl grew to its full height and would sit on the mantelpiece all day before flying off for a night's hunting.

The magpie grew to be a magnificent bird, with a deep blue sheen and long, elegant tail-feathers. He would spend all day at the top of the trees in the garden, flying down when called to land on my shoulder, and roosting in the shed every night. He would hide things in holes,

'The magpie grew to be a magnificent bird, with a deep blue sheen and long, elegant tail-feathers.'

and then carefully cover the hole with bits of paper, banging the paper down thoroughly with his beak. We never found one sixpence he hid. The children gave him a toy pipe from a cracker and he would strut about with the pipe in his beak. He could open a box of matches in a few seconds, holding it with his claws and knocking one end of the inner box with his beak, until all the matches spilled out.

I was very sad when he disappeared; he was so tame that he would hop onto anyone's hand, and I hoped that whoever took him from the garden didn't put him into a cage. We had tried to let him live as natural a life as possible for a bird that seemed convinced it was human.

I recently went back to my village in Cheshire, and noticed that the trees with the rookeries in them are still there, and I wondered whether the people who now live there have the same dilemma every spring.

I do know and understand the arguments against keeping wild things as pets. But I still say — what do you do when children bring you a pathetic ball of wet feathers? And if the bird survives, how do you convince it that it's not a member of the family and must go out into the world? □

Kittiwake

> Kittiwake! Kittiwake!
> the sea-bird mews —
> bad news on the home front,
> pecking like Cain with his beak
> Mark 1 chick has pushed Mark 2 chick
> Death to the runt! Death to the runt!
> over the top of the nest —
> Kittiwake! Kittiwake! the sea-bird cries
> Siblicide! the birdman sighs.

Michael Henry

67

HUGH BARRETT

My affair with the duchess

Drawing by Anne Roper

MY YOUNG BROTHER once accused me of having an affair with a duchess. He was right, in a way. I was young and very susceptible to feminine charms. The duchess — grand duchess in fact — had them in abundance: twinkling eyes, silky hair, the whitest shoulders, nicely rounded where she should be, and a disposition gentle, warm and friendly.

I was managing a remote farm in north Essex, living all alone in a small thatched house, distant even from the farm buildings. Among my pleasures was to look after a small herd of pedigree Essex Saddleback pigs. Now I happen to like pigs. I always have, from the moment they emerge as slippery squealers to the time they arrive on the breakfast table.

This is where I come clean about the grand duchess. She was an Essex gilt. I once heard a farming lady tell her daughter: 'A gilt, darling, is a girl pig not old enough to be married.' Not absolutely accurate, but near enough.

The grand duchess had not only the virtues I have described, but breeding that was quite impeccable. Her full title was Debenham Grand Duchess III. In the normal course of events I wouldn't have taken any special notice of her, but she fell sick. Her siblings started to bully her. She had her tail bitten to the bone and that simply would not do. So I moved her to a pen on her own, and personally fed and watered her, tickled her behind the ears, scratched her back and said sweet things to her, not realising how attached to me she was becom-

'She would push her nose forward to sniff the wind ... and make appreciative little squeals the faster we went. ...'

ing. In a short time she managed to escape her pen and follow me round the farm, snuffling and rooting for things to eat.

One day she caught me unawares and jumped into my car. That's when I ought to have seen the way things were going and called a halt to the affair. But I didn't. She wasn't snobbish: she sat with me on the front seat and, with the windscreen open (those were the days when they could be opened), she would push her nose forward to sniff the wind, ears pricked and alert, eyes sparkling, and make appreciative little squeals the faster we went.

It didn't stop at car rides. She took to coming home for tea, stayed for supper — and, as it was too far to take her back to her pen, she stayed the night. She tried following me upstairs but I wasn't having that and she had to make do with the hearthrug.

This could not go on. My girlfriend complained that the car smelled, which was a gross calumny, for the grand duchess was clean as a whistle and sweet as a nut. It became a case of 'either she goes or I won't come' — and the girl won.

I missed the duchess but, by the time the break was made, she had developed to the stage when she must take up life's task. She was introduced to a rather elderly but splendidly-bred fellow: Barling Dictator XV, whose forebears had won championships all over the country. The meeting was most successful. Barling Dictator played his part vigorously and in due time Debenham Grand Duchess III produced ten splendid youngsters, all alike as peas in a pod.

After that we rather lost touch. I hope she was happy. I was, for once I had cleansed the car the girlfriend became a fixture.

All this was 50 years ago, and looking back there are some things I regret. I shall never see an Essex pig again. The breed was amalgamated with the Wessex Saddleback — an inferior breed in my opinion, with no white on the hind legs nor to the tip of the tail. They became the British Saddleback and that, too, has vanished into the pens of rare breeds.

It was about that time, too, that breeders gave up bestowing on their animals the grand titles that were once so common. You can go from one end of the country to the other and never meet a grand duke or duchess, nor even a countess. Less noble but just as romantic, titles such as Lavenham Lilac or Manningtree Moonrise — both of which feature in my diaries as splendid dams — will never be heard of again.

Nowadays, they just get numbers in stainless-steel ear-clips. □

Wild life and tame

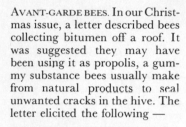

Edited by Euan Dunn

AVANT-GARDE BEES. In our Christmas issue, a letter described bees collecting bitumen off a roof. It was suggested they may have been using it as propolis, a gummy substance bees usually make from natural products to seal unwanted cracks in the hive. The letter elicited the following —

The practice of using propolis substitutes is not exceptional as bees readily improvise. A retired county bee-officer tells of bees in treeless areas of the West Country collecting tar from roads to use as propolis. In the era before household rubber-gloves, this resulted in the beekeeper transferring the tar to otherwise pristine combs of honey in the course of handling them.

Bees are equally opportunist at finding honey-making materials. During the Second World War, when sugar and honey were scarce, a bee-keeper whose garden backed on to a small soft-drinks factory watched his bees do a half-roll out of the hive and into the windows of the factory, to return with loads of 'flavour-of-the-day' syrup to convert into honey. This he sold readily to customers, and then bought proper honey from a nearby bee-keeper for his own use.

In the 1950s, when I was managing hives in an urban cemetery, I noticed groups of cells of bright red and green 'honey'. The gravedigger pointed to a nearby table-jelly factory, and gave me a graphic account of what the workers call the bees! Incidentally, cemeteries are ideal sites for bees, with floral tributes contributing to the year-round pollen supply. When St. Katharine Docks in London were redeveloped, the lady architect included trees and shrubs from all over the world, and added beehives. An eminent bee-keeper, Mr Les Wale, whose office overlooked the dock, was co-opted to assist, and eventually won some prizes with the honey. Mr Wale never told the judges the source of the unusual flavour, which arose from the bees sipping dregs from Coca-Cola cans in the dockside litter-bins. Another set of hives I attended in London produced a good crop of very pale honey, from gleanings in the Tate & Lyle sugar refinery about quarter of a mile away. What price 'pure' honey? — *H. W. F. Embling, Forest Gate, London E7.*

▷▷

71

A tawny owl brings a young rat (left) and (below) an earthworm (common prey on wet nights) to her nest in an ancient yew in north-east Derbyshire. Photographs by Jim Russell (see 'The Storm Owls' below).

Just after the Second World War, Cecil Tonsley, the well-known bee-keeper and then, as now, editor of *The British Bee Journal*, had a top-floor office in Gough Square off Fleet Street. The surrounding bomb-sites produced a rare assortment of flora and quite a good honey crop for the bee colonies which Cecil kept on the rooftop. The bees, however, being unable to find any resinous trees in the area, sealed the edges of their combs with black tar from the road surface. The honey appeared perfectly clean and was unaffected by the tarry substitute for propolis. — *Charles Parlett, Wivenhoe, Essex.*

Some races of honey-bees, notably the Caucasian, collect considerably more propolis than others. At the Government research station at Rothamsted, Hertfordshire, we found bees collecting not only various resinous substances from trees but also partially solidified tar, varnish, and paint that had softened and become workable on hot days. Such propolis is used by the western honey-bee not only for stopping up cracks in the hive but also to varnish all parts of the hive's interior and to cover up such intruders as mice that they have killed and which are too large for them to remove. It is interesting to note that Stradivarius is reported to have used propolis from beehives for varnishing violins. — *Colin Butler, Cambridge.*

THE STORM OWLS. I had spent the previous five days slowly building a hide in a yew-tree, 20 feet off the ground and ten feet from the hole in the trunk where the owls had chosen to rear their young, now over a week old. Getting into the hide meant a climb up the main trunk. A ladder would have made life easier, but I didn't want to leave one around for anyone else to find, so instead I kept a hidden length of rope. I tied one end to the camera bag, climbed the tree and then pulled up the gear. This time no female flew out, suggesting that the young were now old enough to be left unattended for longer periods.

But I decided not to check. Tawnies have been known to attack fiercely anyone showing too much interest in their young and, as they are silent fliers, such attacks are without warning. Once I had set up the camera and put two flash units outside the hide, I sat quietly and before long I could hear the muffled sounds from inside the nest-hole. All was well. As dusk approached, the hunger calls of the young grew louder. Suddenly the drawn-out call of a tawny owl sounded from the far side of the wood, answered by the female's sharp 'keewick'. Excited noises from the young anticipated their first food of the evening. A dark shape ghosted across the sky and, sensing rather than seeing that the owl was perched at the nest-entrance, I pressed the shutter release, lighting the scene for a split second.

Another instant and it had flown off, having delivered its prey, which the resulting photograph showed to be a young rat (left).

After the third such visit, the adult (which I took to be the female) stayed to brood over the young for several hours. I think she knew what the weather was going to be like for the rest of the night. Just after midnight, I detected a distant rumbling in the west which increased in intensity over the next hour. Just when it seemed to have passed over, the heavens opened. The thunder was deafening, and lightning split the darkness every few minutes, making me thankful I had not used my steel scaffolding tower. The rain continued long after the electric storm had passed, but with the first light of dawn it gave way

to a fine drizzle. A skylark started singing and soon there was light enough to let me lower the equipment and cautiously make my way down the slippery branches. — *Jim Russell, Chesterfield, Derbyshire.*

BIRD-FEEDER HYGIENE. I once contacted the late Bruce Campbell (who used to edit these pages) to describe the sick and dying finches among those coming for food we put out. His concern was brisk and immediate, and his advice sound: 'It's almost certainly salmonellosis. You must clean up your site first.' He told me how to do this, and to stop feeding the birds for a while. It was a hard step, but we faced down the puzzled birds and went on denying them. It is our impression that there is much less salmonellosis among finches now but, if we do see any, we shall scald the drinking trays and nut containers, mow the grass, and think of Bruce Campbell who took away our feeling of helplessness. I also like to think that some Oxfordshire farmers have adopted more hygienic practices that lessen the risk to finches that feed around their farms. — *Evelyn Maddock, Oxford.* [According to Chris Mead of the British Trust for Ornithology (BTO), local outbreaks of salmonellosis are still not uncommon. The main victims are greenfinches, chaffinches, and house sparrows, sometimes also dunnocks, but seldom tits. It arises from one or two infected birds defecating on artificial feeding- or drinking-sites which have been in use for some time. Suspended feeders are less at risk than tables and ground-sites, because the droppings land away from the feeder. If you feed birds on the ground, vary the sites. As Bruce recommended, periodically clean and scald feeders and tables. Do likewise if the ground surface is hard, or — in the case of grass — keep it mown short. If you come across a lot of sick or dying birds, contact your local veterinary (or MAFF) officer, since there may be some other cause like an agricultural spray. As for hygiene on farms, finches have much more to fear from the catastrophic effects of 'clean' farming methods on the availability of weed seeds in the fields. Losses of these caused by herbicides have brought massive reductions in recent years in the likes of linnets and skylarks. — *E.D.*]

MONOCHROME TORTOISESHELL. Early in May, I noticed a butterfly sunning itself, wings outspread, on aubretia in the front garden. It was the same size and shape as a small tortoiseshell but its wings were shiny silver and slate grey, except for a faint orange-and-black blob on either side of the thorax, and on the forewing. I would have taken a photograph, but the butterfly was too flighty, only once relanding on some nearby arabis before flying off, never to be seen again. There was nothing similar to it in my books. If it was a small tortoise-shell, is this colour deviation unusual? Why does it occur? — *Pamela Johnson, Durham.* [Pamela enclosed an excellent colour drawing of the butterfly, indicating that it must surely have been an aberrant small tortoiseshell. According to Dr Jeremy Thomas, colour variation in this species can be quite extreme, ranging from dusky to very bright, and arising from exceptionally high or low temperatures during development. Apart from sometimes occurring in the wild, freaks can easily be produced in captivity by rearing chrysalides at different temperatures. — *E.D.*]

PERSISTENT BLACKBIRDS. My untidy back garden measures about 15 × 25 yards and is bounded on three sides by privet-hedges. In most years, blackbird, thrush or dunnock breed successfully. The cock of last year's pair of blackbirds was easily recognisable by a drooping wing. The saga began on 10 March when I saw his mate carrying material to a trimmed yew-tree, a nest-site often used in the past. The nest was never completed. Her second nest was in a privet near the compost heap and got as far as three eggs before being abandoned, probably as a result of a feral cat which sometimes sleeps on the heap. The third nest was built high up in a pyracantha, and eggs certainly hatched because I saw both parents carrying food to the nest. Then, early one morning, I dis-turbed a magpie from above this nest, and that was the end of that one.

The fourth try was again in one of the privet-hedges. At least two eggs were laid and then stolen, again probably by magpies. Yet another privet was chosen for nest five, and this was successful, fledging three young which were fed around the garden, by the cock on its own, for about 18 days. Meanwhile, the hen refurbished nest five and laid a new clutch which also hatched. I never managed to count how many fledged but the saga ended with the cock feeding at least one fledgling as late as 24 July. In mid-August, the cock reappeared after an absence and was busy chasing young blackbirds away from windfall apples and at last feeding himself. — *Ernest Hinchliffe, Lincoln.* [Providing the summer is wet enough (to guarantee a good worm supply) blackbirds can raise two or three broods, sometimes (as shown here) after several abortive attempts. Typically, the cock tends fledglings, while the female is renesting, the young taking up to three weeks to reach independence. Their responsibilities over, the adults go into purdah for a complete body moult, explaining this cock's disappearance till mid-August. — *E.D.*] □

Moon in the mill

by James Frank *Photographs by the author*

NIGEL MOON loves windmills — 'Because they're there,' he says with a blue-eyed smile, his laughter-lines accentuated by a fine dusting of flour.

Nigel runs Downfield Mill, a two-sailed tower-mill, which the twentieth century has besieged with bungalows and vegetable patches in the flat, flat fields of Cambridgeshire outside Soham. From its 100ft high top the views are across fecund miles of beet and wheat to Ely Cathedral.

Nigel grinds rye, oats, wheat, maize and barley. About 60 per cent of his product is a range of additive-free strong, wholemeal bread-making flours which are popular with people who want healthy eating and more flavour than they get from the factory produce. White flours make up the other 40 per cent.

The miller's compact, restless figure clatters up and down the vertiginous stairs which link the mill's five floors, as he checks, fills, ties and shifts sacks. It is not quite a one-man job because Nigel's mother, Ruth, a lively 70-years plus, helps out from time to time especially when the mill is open on Sundays and queues form (admission is 70p or 30p for children).

Nigel always wanted a mill and he managed to buy Downfield in 1975. It was built in 1726 as a smock-mill (wood instead of the present brick). A gale wrecked it in 1887 and it was rebuilt in its present form. When Nigel

Maintaining his 268-year-old mill at Soham, Cambridgeshire, is a perpetual challenge to its owner, Nigel Moon. You are more likely to catch him fiddling with the fantail (opposite above), than reflecting philosophically on the world from beneath his lucky horseshoe (right).

took over it had not ground floor since the late 1950s when the fantail, which sets the sails to the wind, fell off. With the help of a friend and a small but much appreciated grant from the district council, Nigel spent five years restoring it, learning a millwright's skills as he went. By 1980 the stones were grinding again.

It is the functional, mechanical tradition that fascinates Nigel. The fine white dust dances in shafts of light; the rumble of machinery and the soft hiss of moving grain are occasionally punctuated by a bell warning that the hopper needs to be refilled. Here is a simple, robust, living machine performing an elemental job unchanged for centuries. A windmill contains no impenetrable black-box wizardry.

Nigel's greatest pleasure is in making or mending something for the mill which he thought was beyond him. He is proud that he mounted Downfield's new sails weighing a couple of tons each. The mill's maintenance is a continual challenge.

Downfield mills something between a ton-and-a-half and two tons of flour each week. It is sold mostly in the

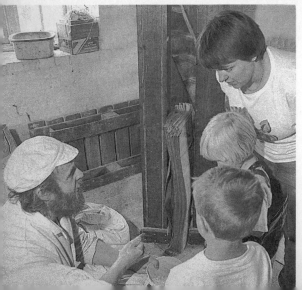

Being a windmill buff, Nigel Moon loves to show visitors around (Downfield mill is open on Sundays) and to explain the simple, ancient mechanics of the business to them.

East Midlands where Nigel spends much of the week delivering orders. He is always on the lookout for good, convenient markets local to the mill. The mill is his only living; he uses the word 'living' wryly.

A mere 12mph of wind turns his sails, so he is frustrated when he has to use the auxiliary engine. 'You could do that in the garden shed', he says, tugging at a temporarily grey beard. But almost as frustrating is the rigidity of the grain trade. It is always a problem to obtain grain in quantities smaller than a huge lorry load, when a few sacks at a time is what Downfield needs.

Contemporary Britain has crept up on Downfield mill, originally an eighteenth-century smock-mill.

Another problem, eased somewhat in recent years, is how to sell his by-products — organic bran and the 'middlings', a mixture of bran and coarse flour — which come from the Downfield style of milling. A useful outlet is a farm near Ely called Naturally Yours which feeds his bran to its organically reared pigs. Individual customers sometimes take the middlings for use in pastry.

Nigel thinks Cambridgeshire people are lucky to live among one of the country's most important concentrations of windmills — smocks, towers and posts — in the country, but then he is an enthusiast. Running up and down those stairs between the ground floor, the bin floor, the bin-charging floor and the dust floor, fighting for an economic niche for quality, he needs to be. □

History from the ground

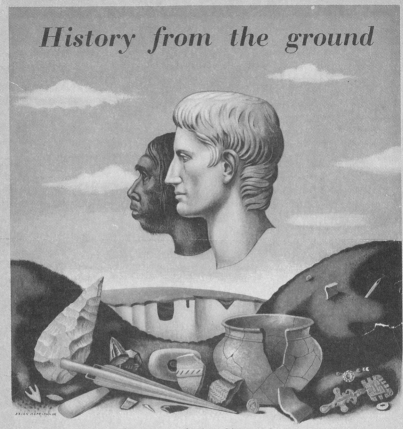

Ancient pottery fragments and other objects such as
these may be found wherever we dig into the ground.
They alone can tell the story of mankind before history was
written. Watch for them and bring likely finds to expert attention.

by Christopher Hall

AROUND THE END of World War II, when people
dreamed optimistic dreams, Brian Hope-Taylor, a young
archaeologist (later famous as the excavator of Yeavering,
the Beowulf-style hall in Northumberland), typed an

'outline of a Campaign of Archaeological Propaganda' for the nascent Council for British Archaeology. And for it he designed the poster opposite.

Hope-Taylor declared that 'public apathy is the pernicious anaemia of archaeology: it deprives research of the data and financial support which constitutes its bloodstream'. Half a century since the poster was launched and the CBA founded, archaeologists have seen an enormous surge of public interest in what they do. Television brought the dug past into all our homes — often via larger-than-life personalities like Professor Glyn Daniel and Sir Mortimer Wheeler. Suddenly, as housing programmes and new roads advanced, there was a lot more archaeology about.

Since the beginning of the 1970s, government spending on rescue archaeology mounted steadily — from less than half a million pounds a year to around £7m today. There were exciting developments in the presentation of archaeological discoveries, notably of Viking York and Vindolanda on Hadrian's Wall. To an outsider, the profession seemed to be carried confidently on a tide of official goodwill and popular interest. But underneath were tensions, of which the chief were financial. Like any other academic activity, archaeology has always been constrained by the resources available, or not available. Time was when a Victorian gentleman with a penchant for antiquities was restrained only by how many of his estate workers he could borrow from the farm to dig the local tumulus. Later, money depended on what local authorities and English Heritage and its Scottish and Welsh counterparts could afford. It was never enough, but what was spent was spent essentially at the direction, if not the demand, of archaeologists. Such a relaxed scenario was not to be tolerated by a government noted equally for its parsimony with the public purse, its attachment to market forces and — too often — an ill-concealed philistinism. Thus emerged from the Department of the Environment, in 1991, PPG 16 in a series of official Planning Policy Guidance notes, this one dealing specifically with archaeology.

PPG 16 established for archaeology what had already been established in other arenas where commerce and the environment clash — namely that the polluter should pay. For archaeology this means that the person or company whose activity may damage or bury the archaeological resource should pay for its investigation and the cost of recording what is found and, if need be, of excavating and/or preserving it.

But developers want to get on with the business of building houses or factories or whatever, and selling them or letting them for profit as fast as they can. They don't want to be digging up Romans when they could be digging foundations. So they act as any entrepreneur would, in obedience to the market. They put the archaeological work out to competition; that is now the normal practice. The archaeological units tender for the jobs and

In the spring and summer of 1972, volunteer archaeologists raced against time and the bulldozers to rescue what they could as the M40 ploughed through the Chilterns. Left, a volunteer inspects a late Roman grave at Beacon Hill, now a cutting 150 feet deep in the chalk. One especially frustrating loss was almost an entire Iron Age village. Tragic dramas like these led to increased government funding for rescue archaeology in advance of construction. Picture by Oxford Mail and Times.

The medieval farm being excavated above is at Sadlers Wood on the Chilterns and has lain under the M40 traffic for 20 years now. Picture by D. Burton.

have become very businesslike. They watch costs — and of course they shave costs.

Andrew Lawson is unit director of the Trust for Wessex Archaeology Ltd in Salisbury. He is an archaeologist by training. He is also a businessman at the forefront of the new way of doing things. As his unit's chief executive, he reports to a board of directors who are in turn appointed by trustees. Under its competitive exterior the unit is still a charity, its objects being to advance archaeological knowledge and education as approved by the Charity Commission; making money is not its be-all. Mr Lawson runs a full-time staff of 40. Typically he will put a manager and supervisor (archaeologist) onto a site with anything from two or three to 30 or 40 (depending on the scale of operations) more or less itinerant excavators. A preliminary desk-study of a site may be priced as low as £200; a large-scale dig at hundreds of thousands. His unit's digs currently average around £40,000.

Originally the Wessex unit served the five counties of Berkshire, Hampshire, Wiltshire, Dorset and the Isle of Wight. It still concentrates on that area but, like other such units, it tenders for jobs in all sorts of places. It is in regular competition with, for instance, its neighbours to the north, the Oxford trust. 'We respect each other,' says Mr Lawson cautiously. 'We frown on some things they do, and they frown on some things we do,' but he politely refuses to explain the causes of these wrinkled brows. Apparently there is still honour among archaeologists.

But for how much longer? Two of Mr Lawson's former employees have set up their own archaeological company, with no nonsense about being a charity. Already there are many archaeological consultants who hire themselves out to anyone who will pay their fees.

This can lead to strange situations. Mr Lawson volunteers: 'Many of my colleagues thought I had lost my marbles when I appeared at a public inquiry to support a developer who wanted to build a hotel at Avebury' (the great neolithic henge in Wiltshire). Mr Lawson said that the developer (this was at the end of the 1980s) had made sure that the site was properly examined archaeologically and had modified his plans to protect the archaeological resource. 'He had done everything demanded of him by the archaeological criteria: I was quite prepared to say so on his behalf.'

Other archaeologists were found by opponents of the scheme to disagree with Mr Lawson, which seems bad enough to the innocents among us who think that in these learned matters there is but one truth. But perhaps worse is that Mr Lawson — by sticking so closely to his archaeological brief — appeared to lend aid to a development widely disliked on grounds of the damage it would do to the amenity and ambience of the great monoliths.

One might take this as a cogent example of how easy it

is for archaeologists — having entered the market — to become soulless, hired technicians. That probably would not be fair to Mr Lawson, though he says bluntly enough: 'We must recognise that in the real world there are people who have other uses for land than archaeology and that they are entitled to those uses.' But the archaeologist as the lackey of the developer is a fear haunting a lot of people in the profession.

Richard Morris became director of the Council for British Archaeology in 1991. He is a bearded 47-year-old with wide interests, including music and aviation history, but his specialism is ecclesiastical archaeology. He mixes metaphors with some abandon ('archaeology is a discipline fuelled by research-driven goals'); he is politically incorrect enough to bum a cigarette and to smoke small cigars unblushingly. He works from CBA's office, a sixteenth-century house surrounded by post-war flats in York.

Last November, in the CBA's journal, he sounded the alarm with an article headed 'Archaeology — a casualty of the market?' The CBA's strength is that it represents just about every sort of archaeologist; it turns over £3½m a year and has important publishing and educational roles so, as its paid servant, Mr Morris has to mind his words. He therefore carefully rehearsed all the arguments in favour of the market — efficiency, an end to cost escalation, and the hoped-for Thatcherite trend towards private sponsorship of the arts and scholarship.

But his message is that these arguments don't wash. The market is a false market: 'Many developers neither want nor need archaeology . . . They buy archaeological services because they are unlikely to obtain planning permission if they don't'. Moreover, markets are volatile, 'delivering lurches between feasts and famine'. The modern archaeological trust responds to a recession by laying off staff, thus 'wiping its collective memory'.

This might not matter if we could be sure that the

curatorial archaeologists (as opposed to the ones who do the digging) were in a position to preserve the memory and the purity of the discipline. But they work in bodies like English Heritage, and its Welsh and Scottish counterparts, and in local government where they look after the vital SMRS (sites and monuments records). The local authority archaelogists, especially, face a fragmented future as reorganisation looms and they don't have money enough anyway. And though they may set archaeological criteria for a site, they are not, says Mr Morris pointedly, in a position to police the contracts between the units and the developers. If corners are being cut, they may not be able to prevent it; they may not even know it.

Richard Morris calls for three things —

First, a recognition that archaeology is about learning. (By implication it is not about helping people to get planning permissions.)

Second, if contract archaeology is here to stay, then it needs consistent funding so that collective memories are not wiped from time to time, and it needs the backing of an effective curatorial branch of the discipline in local government.

Third, the voluntary sector, overtaken now by the professionals, should be revived and enthused.

It is a shrewd analysis of what is necessary. Just as managers in the health service now take decisions once reserved for clinicians, so we may expect to see accountants and finance-directors taking archaeological decisions. They must be disciplined by curatorial archaeologists with statutory duties and volunteers with passions for the past.

Let us hope the CBA will follow its director's lead and be the Conscience of British Archaeology. For markets don't have consciences. □

ARTHUR APPLETON

The charmless Cheviot

Photograph by Arthur Williams

IS THERE A WORSE TOP than that of The Cheviot? It is
not chasms and drops that I'm worried about: the top of
The Cheviot is a plateau, with not a fissure to slip into or
a side to fall from. It's a bog plateau of green and black
slime. A top where to avoid sinking down to your knees,
maybe thighs, you work obliquely, with tactical retreats.

On the border-fence side, you might trip over the
solidified expletives of exhausted Pennine Way walkers
who, nearing the end of their slog, found themselves
drawn conscientiously to The Cheviot's trig point, and
so you could fall flat and extricate your filthy self looking
like a commando ready for a night attack. You could
knock yourself out, I suppose, and drown, enwrapped in
the sludge. Maybe people *have* drowned up there. I looked
around for dirty-white stuck-out arms. What a place!

I'd been told that I'd missed nothing in not having
been up The Cheviot. I climbed it eventually because,
after a lifetime of fell-walking, mainly in the Pennines
and Cheviots, here I was at the age of 76 and I'd been on
the top of every hill in the Cheviots except the name one.

It's unfortunate that people new to walking are drawn
to The Cheviot, because of its name and because it's the
highest in the range and at the head of a fine valley. It
will have finished some for fell-walking for life. It should
have become better known than it is, how miserable the
top is, and how much better are the tops of the neighbouring peaks. The native habit of understatement is
to blame. A couple was coming down towards us: the

chap told us it was 'a bit boggy on the top'. His female companion smiled wanly.

We'd left the car in Harthope Valley at Hawsen Burn and worked up the burn until we reached the fence which seems to streak away south and south-west over Scald Hill to the top of The Cheviot.

While we were having our lunch on Scald Hill, with the main ascent in front, a family of four passed us, wearing trainers but otherwise dressed for a Sunday walk in the park. We, with our experience of the high hills, were overdressed. I asked the young father if they were coming back the same way, or did they intend to continue over the top and down into the high end of Harthope Valley. He said he planned to do the latter. I told him in that case he would need compass bearings from Cheviot to Cairn Hill and from there to the valley, otherwise they could be led into deep border trouble, even into Scotland. He smiled. I felt that he had heard of a compass. He said he had a map for half the area.

There's nothing unusual about this. Why such people don't die of exposure with their children is because they are nearly always out on long days in good weather and are young, and so have the time and energy to find their way back eventually.

When you've put behind you six tops and you're on the plateau with the trig-point pillar in the distance, you'll find that this last top, although on nearly level ground, takes an awful long time to reach.

The trig-pillar, built on a massive pedestal on a slightly raised black earth island, is encircled by a wide ring of slime. There must have been many occasions in bad weather when, faced with this morass of liquid mud of unknown depth, the weary Pennine Way slogger has made a vulgar gesture at the column — if he had the spirit left in him — and turned his back on it. And good luck to him.

But we were there in a spell of sunny days, so we

The summit of The Cheviot (2,674 ft) is no mountain crag, but a vast, desolate bog plateau with the OS triangulation pillar on a dark island in the middle. It is just inside Northumberland; the Scottish border and the Pennine Way pass over the shoulder of the hill.

selected our line, summoned up energy and courage and sprinted for it. The dismal mound was embellished with two lemonade bottles and a white peaked cap. The head and body of its owner were not visible.

Tom Stephenson talked of groughs up there. The word's not in the *Shorter Oxford* but it sounds appropriate. They could be fiends which come out at nights and plodge about the plateau. In fact they are sodden ditches in the peat. Wainwright talks of a sea of squelchy black ooze, and filthy and pathless peat hags that demolish the spirit and defeat the flesh. He is not understating.

Beyond the Ordnance Survey column, amid Wainwright's lumpier peat hags, we made for the boulders on the outhill of Cairn Hill, and then on a compass bearing turned to the long trackless descent to Harthope Burn, stumbling downhill on huge grass tufts like giant dismembered heads (grough's heads, no doubt) with hidden depth of ground in between. It's a descent designed by nature to twist knees and ankles.

Keep The Cheviot for punishment. ☐

'Come back! Now's your chance to do something great!'

Nature v. Art

Reg Finbow

goes sketching with the open-air class

'If that tree spoils the composition — leave the **** thing out.'

'Today, we have painting by numbers. One, shut up. Two, select subject . . .'

'Well, I think it's OK. I'm coming to be a naïve painter.'

Stoatal war...

Photographs by **Derry Argue**

These stoats were engaged in a fierce tussle on a farm road at Tarland, near Ballater in Grampian last August, when Derry Argue passed by in his car. Luckily he was equipped with camera and telephoto lens. The stoats had each other by the neck and head and were twisting over and over so rapidly that even $1/1000$ sec shutter speed could not completely freeze the action. So engrossed were they that the photographer got within a few yards before they noticed him and took off, still biting each other on the neck as they went.

This was probably a territorial encounter, rarely witnessed because stoats defend very large territories (perhaps as much as 25 acres) and usually demarcate boundaries with musky anal-scent-gland secretions and sometimes urine.

It is hard to see from these photographs which sex is involved. Males are bigger than females and also defend bigger territories. A loose harem system operates such that a male stoat may have one or more female territories within his own. Males often defend their own territory against other males, while each female defends hers against other females.

Possibly this fight was not between adults, but juveniles which disperse in July and August, males more than females, to establish their own territories. Juveniles also indulge in play-fighting, but the encounter shown here has the hallmarks of a serious altercation.   **Euan Dunn**

CLEONE SIMONS

Living with leeks

Drawing by Ionicus

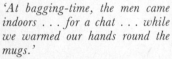

'At bagging-time, the men came indoors ... for a chat ... while we warmed our hands round the mugs.'

THE GARDENING BOOKS go to great lengths to describe how best to grow leeks — holes with a dibber, filled up with water; trenches, earthing-up.

There was none of that nonsense when I was working on a north-east Cheshire market-garden during the war. My family and I love leeks, but at that time of my life I had a surfeit of them. Sweet williams, scabious and asters were being run down; production of leeks was being stepped up. They had always flourished in the damp, cool climate there, so obviously they were a good, safe crop which did not require complicated cultivation or pest control. The fields were simply ploughed and harrowed over with a liberal spread of farmyard manure together with some bag-muck; the soil was already black and rich with a fine tilth from generations of market-gardening. Seeds were sown in March in frames and planting was in early summer. The seedlings were forked

out and laid carefully in barrows as, one bright morning, Tom and Harry, the men, sallied forth with spades, accompanied by Brian the lad, and me the girl.

A line was pegged across the field and off we went. Brian and I had to drop the fiddly plants at suitable intervals, starting from opposite ends of the line, each closely followed by a planter, who was amazingly quick and continually on our heels. Harry and Tom just made a slit with their spade, slide in the leek plant, and then put their feet on the soil to firm it in. They built up a swift, rhythmic movement and never seemed to tire.

Those were lovely days: the smell of the young leeks to sharpen our appetites mixed with the delicious aroma of newly-turned soil. When bagging-time came round, we were always ready for the jug of hot, sweet tea which was brought out to us while we munched our cheese sandwiches. Being agricultural workers, we received — and

95

needed — an extra cheese ration.

Once planted, the leeks were left to get on with growing. No need to water them in — the climate saw to that. Frames and greenhouses were degged, but crops in the fields, never.

As autumn changed into winter, it was time to harvest the leeks which had now grown plump and succulent. Friends often commiserated because they thought I had to work out in all weathers, but this was not the case. Certain jobs had to be done outside regardless, but our boss was very thoughtful and if he could arrange for us to do our work in a warm greenhouse or shed, he would gladly do so. We were not expected to stand if we could sit to a job, either. Tom and Harry would go out into the field and lift the leeks, while Brian would pick up the piles, put them on a large barrow and wheel them over the road and up the yard to the bunching-shed.

Here all was warmth and cosiness; it was about 12 feet square and concrete-floored. In a corner stood a small, iron coke-stove whose black pipe ran up through the roof and which blasted out heat most efficiently.

This shed was my domain, shared at times with the boss and his pleasant wife; they were middle-aged but we all got on well together. The soft, black soil had been knocked off the roots by the men in the field; our job in the shed was to trim the leeks and make them presentable and appetising for the next day's market. All discoloured outer leaves had to be pulled off and thrown on the floor, together with trimmings from any long leaves, and then we could place the leeks neatly in their wooden boxes. When the men had got up sufficient leeks, they joined us in the shed.

None of this was very arduous; it was the smell of the leeks that was so disagreeable. As the pile of squishy leaves on the floor grew higher and the stove pushed out more heat, the atmosphere in the shed grew ever more noxious. It was with some relief that we saw Brian com-

ing over with another load, as we knew that we should
have a breath of fresh air while he swept and forked out
the droppings and took them to the muck-midden, as
market-gardeners call the compost heap.

Onions and garlic are reputed to be good for colds and
sore throats. If their close relation is imbued with the
same properties, no virus could possibly have survived in
that shed; thinking about it, we did all keep remarkably
fit. The Romans believed that leeks improved the timbre
of their voices; perhaps that is why we enjoyed the sing-
songs with which we enlivened our trimming when the
men joined us.

For those outdoors, frosty days were the most unpleasant. If it had been raining or snowing, the leaves were
full of ice which fell into our hands; the leeks themselves
were frozen solid and were very chilly to handle. I tried
to wear gloves but it was impossible to wield the knife
as well, so I gave it up as a bad job. The gloves also
provoked ridicule from the men, who considered such
precautions a silly affectation, possibly slowing down my
work. On these cold, dry days I often longed to be outdoors with them; in the open fields the leeks did not smell
nearly so strongly and the rhythmic exercise would have
warmed my hands and feet. Gloves would have been no
impediment either — I would have ignored the men's
teasing.

But no, men's and girls' work was firmly divided; in
the stuffy, malodorous shed I had to stay, my feet chilled
by the concrete floor and my hands almost senseless with
trimming frozen leeks. I never felt like socialising in the
evening of a leek day; my hands were so impregnated
with their smell that I felt very self-conscious about giving
offence. At bagging-time, the men came indoors and
sat on the bench for a chat and lots of merry badinage
while we warmed our hands round the mugs. They never
seemed unduly tired for, in the tradition of agricultural
workers, they did not rush. No one ever panicked or ran

hither and thither; they just kept working steadily and all the jobs eventually got done.

The rich, dark fields have now been built on and the old market-gardeners have gone. Some younger ones moved out further into Cheshire but, sadly, are finding costs of production too much for them to compete with foreign growers.

Our leeks never compared in size with the mammoths grown for show in Durham and Northumberland, under overnight guard and boosted by special concoctions. But I'm sure St. David would have approved, even though the more salubrious daffodil has long superseded the smelly old leek as a buttonhole on his name day.   □

Bagging: provisions, especially those taken to work in the field, a word once common from Cumbria to Shropshire.
Deg: to sprinkle, north-west English dialect.

Blackthorn blossom

> Buttermilk white,
> thick as cream,
> and from a distance,
> sweet as a drift
> of wood smoke.
>
> I plunge my face
> into the scented petals,
> and drunken bees
> fall about like
> punters on a pub-crawl.   *John Bond*

SURE NOW? Extract from the minutes of the Staffordshire County Council's rights-of-way liaison group: 'Resolved that the minutes of the meeting held on 9 November 1992 be confirmed with the following amendment: page 2 (minute 20) "Planning permission was being bought" be changed to read "planning permisson was being sought". — *Kate Ashbrook, Turville, Buckinghamshire.*

Tail Corn

From Devon ...

COUNTRYMAN, asked why no tramp ever came to his out-of-the-way village: 'Why, 'cos there bain't nowheer yur vur 'em to go to vrom.'

VERGER in Dartmoor church, to visitor admiring the large carved bosses on the oaken altar rails: 'Don't 'ee touch they there knobs, they be 'oly knobs. Bishop be short-sighted, an' when 'er were 'ere last time, 'er confirmed two o' they.'

OLD farmer, asked if he had ever thought of growing melons in the greenhouse of which he was very proud: 'No, they be wat'ry things. Oi loikes onnins; more taste to 'em.'

WOMAN, comparing notes with friend on their experiences in the local hospital: 'Yiss, us would 'ave been gone if us 'adn't 'ave went.'

OLD gardener, shocked at the amount of money spent on flowers taken to the cemetery: 'Du what yu can for 'em when they'm aloive, Oi says, but don't be decoratin' of 'em up when they'm dead. Bain't no sense tu it.'

VILLAGE woman, relating how she had bested a neighbour in an argument: 'An' when I told 'er as 'ow I noo 'er weren't tellin' the truth proper, a look of stagnation came over 'er!'

DARTMOOR woman, to visitor: ''Ere, my dear, you'm gettin' so thin us 'ns could spit through 'ee.'

SHOP assistant, looking out at the rain: 'Fair gives 'ee moolli-groobs [stomache-ache], doan't un?'

The much-loved Tail Corn column first appeared in The Countryman *more than 40 years ago. This selection by Lynne Borrett is from 1949–1956.*

The town hall at Llantwit Major was built in the fifteenth century, to replace an earlier structure sacked by Owain Glyndwr. The ruins of the Raglan Chantry beside the church (right) are now a memorial garden.

Little town of St. Illtyd

Photographs by **Graham Bell**

In the rural heart of South Glamorgan, the ancient town of Llantwit Major (Llanilltud Fawr in Welsh) is only one and a half miles from the Bristol Channel and well detached from the industrial belt of South Wales. In the fifth century, Illtyd came here from Brittany and set up a monastic community that has been called the first British university; the place became famous throughout the Celtic church as a centre of learning and piety. It so continued until the Norman Robert Fitzhamon took over in 1090. He ruined the community by giving its lands to his followers and to Tewkesbury Abbey, which he founded. Today, the town is largely unspoilt and rich in antiquity. ▷▷

The church of St. Illtyd at Llantwit Major was begun in the twelfth century and added to over the next 300 years. Part of it is a museum of early stones and monuments. There are several pre-Norman crosses, including that of Howel ap Rees (left), a ninth-century ruler, set up by his son Hovelt. ▷

In the church is this memorial (right) to Ruth Hopkins, in elaborate late-sixteenth-century costume. She died in 1580, possibly in childbirth, for there is an effigy of a baby at her right shoulder.

A mile or so outside the town are the extensive ruins of Boverton Place (right), a fortified manor house that once had stabling for more than 60 horses. The first owner, Roger Seys, married Elizabeth Voss who had been a maid of honour to Queen Elizabeth I. They moved into the house at the end of the sixteenth century, but

the family fortunes faded and the house was abandoned in 1766 and has been derelict ever since. Other notable residences near Llantwit Major include the Great House (right) on the road to Cowbridge. This was built in the late sixteenth century and is in fine state today, after having fallen into disrepair between the wars. The Old Grange to the west of the church was built in the thirteenth century, but all that is left of it now is a gatehouse and dovecot (left). ☐

AT THE HEART of the great panorama above in
Britain's premier national park, the Peak District, is
Losehill Hall (arrowed), where readers of *The
Countryman* will be spending a super-value week
this summer, exploring the countryside with ex-

perts, learning about its problems, or just plain enjoying themselves.

Losehill Hall — now the national park's holiday and study centre — is a very comfortable former industrialist's mansion set in its own parkland close to Castleton village. Footpaths lead straight up the hill behind to the Mam Tor ridge with its Iron Age fort and to the massif of Kinder to the north (snow-strewn in our picture, but not, we hope when we are there).

I have booked Losehill Hall exclusively for *Countryman* readers for the week of 27 August–2 September. Full board for six nights plus transport for daily expeditions and rambles will cost £250. From personal experience I commend the good food and the comfort of Losehill Hall. The staff are lovely people; there is a library, a sitting-room combining ease and elegance, a bar — plus lots of easy-to-take-in information about the surrounding national park.

To help us enjoy the week we shall have a string of guests to talk to us (but you don't have to go to their talks if you don't want to — Losehill Hall is Liberty Hall), most of whom write or have written for *The Countryman*. **Humphrey Phelps**, *The Countryman*'s farmer from the Forest of Dean, will talk about his kind of farming; **John Riddall**, the local Ramblers' secretary, will give us a fascinating view of his home country from the footpath; local **National Trust** rangers will explain how they try to conserve wild moorland for millions; **Roland Smith**, the national park's information chief will discuss the perils of too much or too little publicity for the Peak. On the Bank Holiday Monday there is the Hope Show, a mile down the road — and not to be missed.

Interested? Send off your stamped and addressed envelope now to *The Countryman*, Sheep Street, Burford, Oxon OX18 4LH marking your letter LOSEHILL. We'll send you full details. First come, first served. I shall be there and I hope to see you there. — *Editor*.

Countryman's bookcase

Murphy's Law

by Christopher Hall

Men who get out of their groove are rare these days, but this author is one such. He took his degree in mathematics and mathematical physics. He represented his country at a chess Olympiad and was later national champion in the game. He was a founder member of his country's meteorological service and ultimately its director for 14 years. He specialised in agricultural meteorology and was briefly seconded, under a United Nations scheme, to study the links between the weather and the potato blight *phytophthora infestans* which was ravaging Chile in the mid-1950s. This experience led him to study one of the most tragic and dramatic events in his own nation's history.

Patrick Martin Austin Bourke was born in 1913 at Dungarvan, Co. Waterford, his father being a station master on the Great Southern & Western Railway; he took his degree at University College, Cork and proceeded to the career described. The Chilean visit set him considering the great Irish famine of the mid-1840s, caused by the same disease. Now, three decades of his articles, lec-

tures and an academic thesis on the blight — its causes and spread, the Irish dependence on a single crop and how the famine was tackled — have been brought together in **'The Visitation of God?'**, edited by Jacqueline Hill and Cormac Ó Gráda (Lilliput, £20).

If the blight was indeed — in the words of a contemporary coroner's inquest — 'a visitation of God', it was a most effectively and maliciously organised one. It was first spotted in Belgium early in 1845, though its fungal wind-blown nature was missed by most observers. It did not reach Ireland until late in the year, when it could do relatively little harm. And the British prime minister, Robert Peel, then in the last months of power, acted decisively by shipping in North American maize, an early and highly unorthodox piece of famine relief.

Next year things were worse — and more orthodox. The blight was in full fury. In 1845 Sir Charles Trevelyan, assistant secretary to the Treasury, had written to Edward Pine Coffin (of all impossible names!), Commissary-

General in Ireland: '. . . *coûte que coûte*, the people must not, *under any circumstances*, be allowed to starve'. In 1846, serving a new master, the laid-back Lord John Russell, he closed down the relief operation he had so efficiently mounted. A great Irishman, Edmund Burke, was quoted in support of the do-nothing policy: the laws of commerce were the laws of God and to interfere with them, e.g. by buying maize to relieve hunger, was immoral.

The fact is, that over most of Ireland, the average landless labourer's consumption of potatoes was something between 14lb and 18lb *a day*. The tuber was not merely the staple diet, it was the overwhelming monopolist of the diet. When it went down before the blight, so did the people. Between 1845 and 1851, Ireland's population collapsed, through death and emigration, from an estimated 8,500,000 to 6,550,000, leaving an immense, indelible legacy of bitterness against the English, the landlords and the clergy of the established church.

It has been Patrick Bourke's chosen task to illuminate the origin of this legacy — a task here accomplished with erudition, clarity and passion.

From tors to fens

by Kate Ashbrook

The jacket-flap of **Heathercombe, The History of a Dartmoor Valley** (Westcountry Books,

£12.95) by Claude Pike, OBE, DL, MA, LLM (Cantab), LLD (Hon) Exeter, CBIM (*sic*) boasts of the author's concern for conservation, trees and the Devon countryside. It fails to explain that he is chairman and former director of the mining company Watts, Blake, Bearne & Co Ltd, which has desecrated south-western Dartmoor with china-clay workings. Thus the book is a tad hypocritical.

It describes the history of the Heathercombe valley and hamlet near Manaton on eastern Dartmoor, from prehistoric times. It glosses over the alien conifers that blacken the lower slopes of nearby Hameldown, thanks to a dedication agreement with the Forestry Commission, which Pike (the conservationist) continued when he bought the estate in 1955.

He erected three stones, each with three fishes (the Christian symbol he says — not pike) and the wording, one phrase on each, is: 'Thine is the power', 'and the kingdom', 'and the glory'. Writing curiously in the third person, the author says: 'These stones record the owner's philosophy of man's stewardship; power derived from whatever source, to be exercised responsibly as a steward'. It's a shame he hasn't followed this philosophy when it comes to china-clay mining.

Not surprisingly, the fish-stones do not feature in **Thurlow's Dartmoor Companion** by George Thurlow (Peninsula Press, £14.95);

'The parched grass shrunk back into the dykes where frost waits to suck it dry . . .' — one of the gentle drawings by Helen Hale that illustrate Edward Storey's new book of essays, **The Winter Fens**, reviewed by Kate Ashbrook on p.112.

this chunky book describes many elements of the national park, with sketches by the author, of tors, crosses, churches and other features. It is written by someone who loves exploring, and sharing, Dartmoor, but it is hard to see what purpose it serves when we already have a *richesse* of Dartmoor classics.

Julian Critchley also writes of the land he loves in **Border Lands — Shropshire and the Welsh Marshes** (Peak Publishing, £17.95). David Paterson's spacious colour photos are excellent, and the text, which concentrates on south Shropshire, is short and swinging. It is not clear what area the book aims to cover, for the photos extend beyond the text, from Bridgnorth (spelt incorrectly in the caption) to White Mere near Ellesmere on the Clwydian border.

On the other side of England, **The Winter Fens** (Robert Hale, £12.99) is a chatty description of this haunting landscape and its people. Edward Storey visits the fens' inhabitants and records their memories, sometimes verbatim. He begins and ends evocatively with the swans migrating from Russia, to winter on the fens.

Moving to central England, we come to **Oxfordshire Houses** by John Pilling (Oxfordshire Books/Alan Sutton, £12.99), an authoritative, chronological account with good black-and-white photos. Many of the houses have survived because Oxfordshire was fairly prosperous, so they were well built. The various town and country houses, impressive Palladian mansions and workers' homes, are carefully described and explained.

Birds on the map
by Euan Dunn

For bird-watchers, the most outstanding recent book is surely **The New Atlas of Breeding Birds in Britain and Ireland: 1988—91**, edited by D. W. Gibbons, J. B. Reid and R. A. Chapman (T. & A. D. Poyser, £40) and based on fieldwork organised by the British Trust for Ornithology, Scottish Ornithologists' Club and Irish Wildbird Conservancy. Many will already have the 1976 atlas on their shelves, but this only serves to enhance the value of its successor. For bird distributions are rarely static, and the past 20 years have seen all sorts of changes. Some have been dramatic, like the near-extinction of wryneck and red-backed shrike, and wholesale retreat of corncrake and nightingale, contrasting with the recovery of the peregrine population and spread of the hobby.

The new atlas also reveals less charismatic birds on the move, including the remarkable expansion of siskins through conifer afforestation, and the nuthatch's colonisation of Cumbria and Northumberland. Contractions in the abundance of species like skylark, linnet and corn bunting speak volumes for the toll that modern farming has taken of familiar countryside birds. Overall, the atlas's innovative mapping techniques enable us to gauge the abundance, distribution and changing status of 221 species. For anyone seeking a better understanding of the birds these islands have to offer, the new atlas is a mine of knowledge, easily accessible with its highly attractive, jargon-free treatment.

The atlas also gives population estimates, indicating that Britain's commonest bird is the wren (seven million pairs). That the great tit numbers one-and-a-half million pairs is perhaps one of the least interesting statistics for this species, judging by the wealth of life-history detail assembled by Andrew Gosler in **The Great Tit**, the latest monograph in the Hamlyn Species Guide series (£9.99). To discover why the great tit's dialect names include 'joe ben', 'ox eye' and 'saw sharpener', I recommend **The Oxford Dictionary of British Bird Names** by W. B. Lockwood (OUP, £6.99), a treasury for bird etymologists.

Although bird taxonomy was largely resolved last century, the modern tool of DNA-analysis is suggesting hitherto unsuspected branch lines in the family tree. The authors of this new classification, Burt Monroe jun. and Charles Sibley, recognise 9,702 species worldwide, and have produced a valuable inventory of their Latin and English names in

A World Checklist of Birds (Yale University Press, £35).

So well-studied is the world's avifauna that the discovery of a new species is now a supremely rare event. Just as much adrenalin flows, however, when a species thought to be extinct is rediscovered. A fascinating handbook of such surprises has been compiled for the entire animal kingdom by Dr Karl Schuker: **The Lost Ark: New & Rediscovered Animals of the 20th Century** (Collins, £14.99).

At a personal level, much can be discovered about birds by painting them with as much attention to plumage, posture and habitat as the highly talented Terance James Bond has applied to his selected portraits in **Birds: An Artist's View** (Dragon's World, £18.95). With notes by the artist and supporting text by Rob Hume, this book is outstanding value. I am also a great admirer of Rodger McPhail's soft, yet assured water-colours in Colin McKelvie's **A Country Naturalist's Year** (Swan Hill Press, £19.95), which has a strong Scottish flavour.

But no recent publication has given me more pleasure and stimulation than **Island of Terns** (Quiller Press, £16.95) by Bob Chestney, who was 'warden of Scolt Head' (the book's subtitle) for 36 years till his retirement in 1985. A passion for terns is an odd trait with which I am personally afflicted, along with a few other sufferers, but a real understanding

113

*Nature's architecture: this is Great Staple Tor, one of the drawings with which George Thurlow has liberally illustrated his own new guide, **Thurlow's Dartmoor Companion**, reviewed on p.110.*

of terns is given to fewer still. Bob is one of the few. He learned from his father and, by immersing himself in the field from boyhood, was able to develop Scolt into one of Europe's foremost breeding colonies for terns. This is Bob's autobiography, told with the same mischievous Norfolk humour, wit and enthusiasm that delighted the legions of visitors he hosted at Scolt Head. Every armchair conservationist should read this book to see how it is done.

Collective gardening

by Elizabeth Seager

At last autumn's Blenheim Pal-

ace flower show, I was delighted to see that many nurseries were offering the handsome Victorian dahlia 'Bishop of Llandaff', with fiery scarlet flowers above bronzy foliage. Its current popularity is largely due to the work of the National Council for the Conservation of Plants and Gardens which rescued it from obscurity, as John Kelly points out in **The National Plant Collection** (Ian Allen, £25).

The collections scheme was set up by the NCCPG in 1981 to conserve garden plants — species and hybrids — that might otherwise have been lost to cultivation. Collections of perennials, shrubs, trees and climbers now exist all over the country, in private and public gardens, plant nurseries and botanic gardens — as a reference source for study and an inspiration to keen gardeners.

John Kelly traces the scheme's development, and visits 20 collections large and small, ranging from ferns and figs, to crocuses, campanulas and roses, all tended by dedicated gardeners, some amateur, others professional.

Anyone seriously interested in plants will want to buy or borrow this book; the colour photos are superb and John Kelly argues the case for plant conservation with infectious enthusiasm. **The National Plant Collections Directory 1944** lists 600 collections, and includes details of general opening times, special open days and plant sales, plus information on membership of the NCCPG which now has 41 county-based groups (£2.95 at bookshops; £3.50 inc p&p from NCCPG, The Pines, Wisley Garden, Woking, Surrey GU23 6QB).

The Henry Doubleday Research Association has taken the lead in conserving old vegetable varieties whose survival is threatened by over-zealous EU legislation. It has a seed library of 500 commercially extinct varieties, and display beds of rare vegetables at Ryton Gardens, near Coventry. The 1994 edition of its annual directory **The Veg Finder** (HDRA/Moorland Publishing, £5.99) reads like a hymn of praise to the vegetable kingdom. It pro-

vides sources for 3,000 vegetables, and its mouth-watering descriptions should inspire adventurous gardeners to try some less common varieties before they become extinct. No horticultural or allotment society should be without it.

Further inspiration comes from **Vegetables** (Pan, £17.50), a pictorial feast of 650 varieties — roots, fruits and shoots of every shape, size and texture — with marvellous colour-photos by Roger Phillips and fascinating notes on history and cultivation by Martyn Rix.

Rosemary Verey's *potager* at Barnsley House, Gloucestershire must be the most famous vegetable garden in England, and it is not surprising that she has been commissioned to design others. Two glorious examples appear in **Rosemary Verey's Garden Plans** (Frances Lincoln, £18.99), one for a private Northamptonshire garden, the other designed to educate and delight tourists at Mount Stuart on the island of Bute. Sumptuous colour-photos and detailed water-colour planting plans illustrate these and other designs, including knots, pergolas and scented gardens. Her own garden at Barnsley appears in 40 paintings by Gloucestershire artist Charles Neal, to be exhibited for sale at London's Museum of Garden History, from 16–31 May.

Nigel Colborn's **Short Cuts to Great Gardens** (Conran Octopus, £16.99) is packed with imaginative ideas and practical advice to help impatient gardeners create an established garden in record time, with inspiring colour-photos that make it all look delightfully easy. And anyone who gardens on fast-draining soil will welcome Jane Taylor's **Plants for Dry Gardens** (Frances Lincoln, £18.99), a detailed catalogue of 1,000 drought-tolerant plants, compiled from personal experience of gardening on two acres of shale mine-waste in the Forest of Dean.

New titles in the Ward Lock Master Gardener series include Jane Courtier's **Growing Indoor Plants**, Alan Toogood's **Lawn Craft** and John Mattock's **Growing Roses** (Ward Lock, £5.99 each) — all good-value basic guides, though the last contains some careless captioning. A full-page photo of a white multiflora rambler is labelled as 'Bantry Bay', the large-flowered double pink climber, and a rose captioned as a *rugosa* is almost certainly *Rosa virginiana*.

Farming forebears
by Humphrey Phelps

The diary of Joseph Turrill was found by workmen a few years ago, bricked-up in a cottage wall at Garsington. Edited by Eve Dawson and Shirley Royal, it has now been published as an elegant volume, **An Oxfordshire Market Gardener** (Alan Sutton/ Oxfordshire Books, £14.99). The diary only covers the years 1863– 67 but that is enough to give an inside view of rural life in the mid-nineteenth century. Indeed, it is especially valuable because of this and because it is written in such a lively and readable style. Mr Turrill was in his twenties at this time and courting the girl who later became his wife — a romance which did not always run smoothly. Among the many incidents are the coming of the railway and a smallpox epidemic. The book is of absorbing interest, even the progress of cabbages and beans. By 1880 he had become an enthusiastic photographer and several of his photographs illustrate the book. Turrill, in my opinion, can stand comparison with Kilvert who was his contemporary.

Second Crop by Paul Heiney (Cassell, £14.99) is subtitled *Reflections from a Farmer's Diary*, but it is in a different class altogether. Mr Heiney is a broadcaster and journalist with a hobby smallholding in Suffolk which provides material for his weekly columns in *The Times*, from which this book is a collection. He farms organically and with Suffolk horses; in fact, his is a very old-fashioned way of farming. He has several pertinent observations about modern methods. He strikes me as a sensible sort of man but he will try to be funny, so that all too often the result is a mixture of sense and silliness.

However, he would enjoy looking, as I have, at **Farm Tools and Techniques** by Jonathan

Brown (Batsford, £14.99). It is a photographic record of some of the rural crafts and field-skills belonging to the days when men, and some women too, worked with their hands in the fields. One large photograph shows a newly laid, a perfectly laid, hedge. I would gladly doff my cap to such a craftsman.

I am old enough to have witnessed the last days of this era, when farming was husbandry and there were such craftsmen, and yet young enough to have welcomed the advent of mechanical agriculture, even if I've now come to regret some of it: 50 glorious years of machines, each one more labour-saving, bigger and better than the last.

In words and photographs, Brian Bell has recorded them all comprehensively, in fine style, in **Fifty Years of Farm Machinery** (Farming Press, £18.50). Some have been great boons, but few have lasted long compared to the crafts of earlier days. Aided and abetted by government grants and the banks, farmers have collected the cast-aside machinery like spoilt children with toys.

Set in the days before these machines, **Muck but no Money** by Joyce Wilson (Ellenbank, £5.99) claims to be humorous, fictional tales set in Cumbria. Cumbrian and fictional they may be, but humorous is open to question. Or to put it another way, after reading a couple, I was in no humour to read more.

Sculpting Scotland

by Euan Dunn

As a schoolboy I read that Stornaway, the largest town in the Hebrides and administrative capital of the Western Isles, is Norse for 'the road to the stars'. This discovery of a place-name, at once cosmic and poetic, was just what a teenager in Dan Dare's heyday needed to get hooked on history, but sadly we were taught little of the Viking conquest at school. Would that I had had access then to Anna Ritchie's excellent **Viking Scotland** (Batsford/Historic Scotland, £14.99), which brings alive the six centuries of Norse rule centred in northern Scotland. Sifting evidence from artefacts, buildings and monuments, Ritchie reconstructs everyday Viking life with a rare blend of scholarship and narrative skill. The saga quickly transcends popular images of savagery, showing how the subtler phases of colonisation and trading enriched culture from Scotland to south of the border.

To the mountaineering fraternity at my school in Aberdeen, Torridon in Wester Ross was a fabulous place, our Kathmandu, and the awesome mountain of Liathach its Everest. I remember us poring over the map, trying to conjure an image of Liathach from those contours devouring one another for 3,456 feet, from sea-loch to razor-back summit ridge. Lea MacNally was the National Trust's ranger/naturalist there for 21 years. His **Torridon: Life and Wildlife in the Scottish Highlands** (Airlife Publishing, £17.95), completed just weeks before his death in February last year, is an eloquent celebration of the region, its people, and unique wildlife.

By the time it reaches the coast, 70 miles after leaving Loch Tay, the River Tay has become Britain's greatest river, discharging more water than the Thames and Severn basins put together. In **The River Tay and its People** (Mainstream Publishing, £14.99), Graham Ogilvy, with the help of Graham McKirk's photographs, traces the stream in time and space through the eyes of those who live and work on its banks.

It took the advent of the steam train to usurp the Tay's monopoly on river trade in the last century. The historical background to this emerging force in transport, its achievements and failures, are lovingly recalled in **The Romance of Scotland's Railways** (Thomas & Lochar, £19.95). As in their other joint works, David St. John Thomas and Patrick Whitehouse provide train-lovers with an authoritative, illustrated feast, reeking of soot and scalding steam.

One day, probably in the 1950s, the late Tony Keswick, laird of the wild and remote Glenkiln estate in south-west Scotland, drove to Much Hadham, Hertfordshire, in the vague hope of ordering some brass bath-taps from a bronze-worker he had heard about there. The man turned out to be Henry Moore, and instead of taps Tony Keswick ordered a bronze cast, the *Standing Figure* to place on a flat-topped rock in Glenkiln. Thus began a lifelong friendship and Keswick's vision of putting modern art in a natural setting, the first endeavour of its kind. In **Glenkiln** (Canongate Press, £20), nephew John McEwen tells in words, and John Haddington in haunting photographs, of the powerful tryst created between sculptures and landscape. Instantly these shapes, often so baffling in a gallery, look utterly at home.

Well-tilled words

by Elizabeth Seager

'One of the most pleasing sounds of Springtime to be heard all over the country, is the contented cooing of osteopaths as Man picks up his garden spade,' wrote Oliver Pritchett, quoted in Richard Briers's gardening anthology, **A Little Light Weeding** (Robson Books, £16.95). I know nothing of Pritchett and would have welcomed enlightenment, but dates are missing from too many of the quotations, and there is no index of authors.

That said, it is a most enjoyable read, with its mix of the predictable — Bacon, Cowper, Kipling — and the unfamiliar, including Brother Cadfael's twelfth-century herb garden from an Ellis

'Potting Shed' by Brian Partridge — a detailed and evocative drawing from Mirabel Osler's new anthology, **In the Eye of the Garden**, reviewed on p.120. She calls her garden 'a small calm eye in a world gone mad'.

Peters detective story; moonlit fruit-trees from a Disraeli novel; and hilarious extracts from Joyce Grenfell and *Round the Horne*.

'Lovely morning which we spent clearing ivy off trees' noted the indomitable Queen Mary with satisfaction in her diary for 26 September 1939, at Badminton House. Ivy was her pet hate, and she waged an implacable war against it wherever she went, much to the apprehension of her various hosts.

I enjoyed R. A. Reeves's verses on an old gardener 'stubborn as bindweed, cunning as ivy' (borrowed, without acknowledgement, from the pages of *The Countryman*) and Thomas Hardy's haunting little poem about a garden seat and its nightly ghosts. Jilly Cooper is always fun on class distinctions, not least in the garden, a veritable minefield for the social climber.

No upper-class gardener would allow a garden gnome within his walls, but **The Oxford Book of Garden Verse** (OUP, £17.95) includes a poem by Robert Druce, in which a gnome defends himself as a 'valid, albeit minor, heraldic type', with a proud pedigree stretching back to the kobolds, legendary Germanic dwarfs.

This is just one of many new delights I discovered in this collection of over 200 poems, ranging from medieval to modern, selected and introduced by John Dixon Hunt. Among these flowers and vegetables lurk love, hope, vengeance and murder; and an appropriate end for one old gardener who dies sleeping 'Cold in the sun beside his upright spade', surely the perfect way for any gardener to go.

This is a poet's-eye-view of gardeners, battling with awesome slugs 'bigger than a human eye', and 'white impudence' of ground elder; of railway allotments, greenhouses, back gardens, and the potting shed:

> . . . *a universe*
> *Of unripe pears and golden*
>   *bulbs* . . .
> *warmed and scented by a*
>   *wood-fired stove.*

'Potting sheds should have preservation orders on them,' says Mirabel Osler, who enjoys their smell of 'loam and lime laced with damp mould'. Her other loves include pansies, privacy and winter weather; her hates range from noisy lawn strimmers to 'copybook conformity' in the garden. In ten essays under the title **In the Eye of the Garden**

(Dent, £12.99), she writes with perception, passion and prejudice on topics inspired by her garden — 'a small calm eye in a world gone mad'. It reveals small miracles of nature, sparks off memories of childhood, and life with her husband in Corfu, Thailand and the Shropshire countryside, where together they created a romantic and much-acclaimed garden. Carefully-chosen wood-engravings accompany her reflections. Now widowed, she has embarked on a smaller garden, transforming a flat, bare canvas into a private bosky haven full of 'places to stoop and sidle'.

Morris men
by Derek Schofield

Morris dancers are a familiar sight in villages and towns throughout England — especially the handkerchiefs, sticks and bells of the Cotswold morris of the south Midlands. Yet, since Cecil Sharp toured Oxfordshire and neighbouring counties collecting the dances and tunes which have been the basis for its revival in this century, there has been little attempt to delve deeper into the background and history of the morris.

Sharp's view that the morris was the survival of some 'primitive religious ceremonial', dating back to pagan times and concerned with fertility, has endured. And Sharp was not much interested in acquiring information about the performers.

Keith Chandler, who has now extensively researched the Cotswold morris, has a more down-to-earth approach. This is set out in his two books: **Ribbons, Bells and Squeaking Fiddles: the Social History of Morris Dancing in the English South Midlands, 1660–1900** and **Morris Dancing in the English South Midlands, 1660–1900: a Chronological Gazetteer** (£12.95 and £10.95 respectively, Hisarlik Press for the Folklore Society).

Chandler points out that the first reference to the performance of morris was 1466, which renders theories of pagan origins entirely suspect. Nevertheless, the date is early indeed and no other dance form, at any rate in England, has lasted so long.

'Morris dancing never existed in a cultural vacuum,' writes Chandler, whose work is 'firmly rooted in the social contexts in which it was performed', and he emphasises the participants, the dancers and musicians, 'who have been conspicuously absent from many other studies'. He has painstakingly searched the newspapers of the area, parish records, documents of trades guilds, household accounts and conducted oral research; and *The Chronological Gazetteer* contains all the references which have informed the major study. If any new sources emerge, they will not confound Chandler's observations and conclusions, which must be regarded as definitive.

▷▷

What we find is that morris dancing was mainly performed by young men (and occasionally women) drawn from the agricultural work-force, whose reasons for dancing were a mixture of family connections, status within the community, the desire to travel to neighbouring villages, and the need to supplement their meagre wages.

The events at which dancing took place changed during the period. Initially, dancing occurred at 'Whitsun ales', village festivities held to raise funds for the church. During the last century, these ales were replaced by feast-days for the local benefit societies, and in many places the morris dancers adapted to the new context. The dancers also toured the area (sometimes reaching as far as London), performed at other special occasions, and even met other groups for competitions.

Chandler has identified 151 separate communities which had a morris team. In many cases, the names of dancers have been identified and, in some instances, family trees have been produced, using parish records, to show the relationships between dancers. Two Oxfordshire case-studies, Headington Quarry (where there is still a morris team) and Adderbury (where there is a recent revival) explore the history of morris dancing in more detail.

Ribbons, Bells and Squeaking Fiddles is a definitive, eminently readable study which can be highly recommended, not only to the folk-dance enthusiast, but also to local historians and anyone who has ever stopped the morris dancers on the street and asked 'Where do these dances come from?'

Native hues

by Gilbert Ellice

Lt. Col. Arthur Lloyd-Baker (1883–1979) was an unremarkable Gloucestershire squire of the old school, his home being Hardwicke Court in the village of Hardwicke where his great-nephew still lives. **A Gloucestershire Diarist** (Thornhill Press, £7.95) is his own record of the years 1897–1919 — his time at Eton and New College, and then some eight years as a young country gentleman, hunting, dancing and exercising with the territorials. The last five years are, of course, the war, in which his older brother was killed and he was himself a brave and apparently unquestioning regimental officer.

The value of a diary like this — neatly edited by Joyce Popplewell — is not to be despised, even if the diarist was plainly a very limited personality. In 1912 he reads *Emma* which he dismisses as 'very thin', and in the same year he is cautiously thinking that votes for women might be a good thing, 'but there is the immense difficulty of numbers. I confess I don't want to ruled by a majority of women'. Armistice Day passes with no entry.

He taught modern languages at Cheltenham College for the next 31 years and served for decades as a magistrate and county councillor, including a long chairmanship of the education committee. It is important to know the stuff of which such figures were made.

Whereas Lloyd-Baker was content to suck the same silvery spoon all his life, Joseph Smith (born in 1903 when the squire was in his second year at Oxford) has a tale of compelling social mobility to unfold in **From Plough to College** (Richard Kay, 80 Sleaford Road, Boston PE21 8EU, paperback, £6.95). He was born in Leasingham, Lincolnshire, the son of a landless farm-worker whom he followed onto the land at 14.

Victimised as a trade unionist, he managed to break free and go to the local agricultural institute, then to Ruskin College, Oxford, and ultimately to take a first-class degree in economics and agricultural economy at the University College of Wales, Aberystwyth. This opened the way to a rewarding career in university teaching. His story is full of the insights into life, work and social structure which are missing from the Lloyd-Baker. It is the difference between a couch-potato's life and one lived with purpose.

Today the countryside has few such squires and few such farmworkers, although the image of a countryside so populated is surprisingly persistent. The true

*'Butterfly' by Gertrude Hermes, from **In the Eye of the Garden**, reviewed on p. 120.*

picture of much-ignored poverty, immobility, homelessness and poor public services is competently outlined in **Another Country** by James Derounian, subtitled 'Real life beyond Rose Cottage' (NCVO Publications, £7.95). The author, rural development officer in Northumberland and formerly rural officer with the Devon Community Council, gives us the facts and figures in a pleasantly assimilable form, but he offers no over-arching vision of how the countryside and its suffering communities are to be rescued from the forces now destroying them.

The same goes for **Rural Action**, edited by Paul Henderson and David Francis (Pluto Press in association with the Community Development Foundation and Action with Communities in Rural England, £12.95, paperback). The book is subtitled 'a collection of community work case studies' which range from England to Wales, Ireland and Spain; unfortunately there is no philosophical or political matrix for them.

Another way of looking at the

123

entrails of rural England is the anthropological, which is what we get in **Diverse World-Views in an English Village** by Nigel Rapport (Edinburgh University Press, £30). The publisher claims the book is written 'in an engaging and eminently readable manner' but the opposite is the truth. Mr Rapport spent a year in a south Cumbrian dale doing fieldwork for his doctorate in 1980 and 1981.

Here he is discussing the way Doris (snobbish and discontented farmer's wife) and Sid (macho, Sun-style jack-of-all-trades) talk: 'I wanted to maintain the notion that an appreciation of context was basic to an understanding of what Doris or Sid meant by their words and actions, but add the caveat that the logic behind their behaviour, its wider reference, might be a definition of context which was special and private to them, so that their behaviour might be seen as the result of their recognition in particular events or as a particular situation a further enactment of a particular social context in which they feel that the words and actions of a particular persona would be apposite'. It is a relief to find, embedded in this kind of meaningless cotton-wool, hilarious passages when the author is striving to be invisible or inaudible while the natives — who are implicitly patronised something rotten throughout the book — try to work out what he was up to. ☐

Not what they seem

Cows lift their tails old-fashioned
as tasselled hand-pumps
to deliver semi-liquid pizza pancakes
through organic hatches.

In a field of animals by a quaintly called
stud-farm where there's not a single
cuff or frilly shirt-front in sight
and each of the placid uniformed girls' school
group of cows bears no label
of being Miss Understud.

Michael Kelly

Fifty years ago

Photographs by
W. Ellison and
F. Wilkinson

Half a century ago this spring, these pictures adorned the cramped, sober pages of the wartime Countryman. *Both display the arts of agricultural improvisation. W. Ellison of Carlisle captioned the upper picture 'When the old sow died', but we teamed it with a shot of a hen rearing ducklings and labelled them 'Foster mothers'.*

The caption on the lower picture (by F. Wilkinson of Greenmount, Greater Manchester) was 'A Lancashire farmer's notice', as is apparent from the dialect. Such unofficial path diversions are still common today, but seldom so winningly advertised — 'Keep-out' notices and barbed wire being the norm. — Editor.

Y! CANT I SEE THIS OLE ?
LL ITS LIKE THOWD PATH
R CORNT GET THROUGH
W PATH BEARS TO TREIGHT OER YON

Big savings on motor insurance for over 50s!

You drive a family car
(not a sports or high performance model) ☑

The only drivers are you and your spouse ☑

You (both) are over 30 and under 70 years of age ☑

You (both) have no disabilities and a full licence ☑

You are (both) free of convictions and have had
no accidents in the last three years ☑

If you're a careful driver, stop subsidising the bad risks! Call Commercial Union, you could save £30, £50, even £75 or more!

FREE. This handy car compass is yours
when you request a quote today!

CALL FREE 0800 38 0800

Mon-Fri 8am-8pm, Sat 9am-5pm. Please quote reference number below.
Offer does not apply in Northern Ireland.

COMMERCIAL UNION
Motor and Home Insurance

Ref. no. CM 401

One Countryman to another

by the editor

□ A reader in Berkhamsted, Hertfordshire, **Gwen Stenning**, is 95 years old now, but has vivid memories of her first 'activity holiday' away from home at the age of 18. During the First World War, girls were encouraged to take up farm work that had hitherto been an exclusively male occupation. Miss Stenning became a farm-girl in Devon —

In the summer of 1916, we came across a prospectus for a wartime course in farm-work for women. We were four girls, 18 years old, at home in Hertfordshire. We didn't think of it as war work. Why shouldn't we all go in August, have a lovely holiday, and in three months time be home for Christmas? We applied for the August course and were accepted.

Seale-Hayne Agricultural College — not far from Newton Abbot, Devon — was new just as war came and therefore unopened. It was a practical-looking building, on a hill amid fields — gleaming in the sunshine as we arrived.

Two formidable-looking women in nurse's uniform — medals and all — received us warmly. The larger said she was Matron-in-Charge, and the other was Sister,

her assistant. It was all very nice and friendly and Sister took us upstairs and ushered us into a long dormitory with curtained-off cubicles — just like boarding-school and furnished similarly. We found we were with a very mixed group of 15, both socially and in age.

My pal Win and I examined the beds and found the mattresses were straw-filled and the pillows flock-filled and there were three army blankets — no sheets or pillowcases. Sister had said that the post went at 5pm; our instant letters home included urgent requests for sheets and pillowcases.

Matron and Sister cooked, and the food was of the good plain home variety of those days. But there was no free time or weekend sport or library facilities — no papers and nowhere nearby to go. However, during the week we were quite glad just to sit and go to bed early.

We learnt to milk in the early morning, the cowman instructing us with two cows; he encouraged us by saying they were quiet ones. Stools and buckets were waiting, a large pail of cold water and pads of coarse linen;

udder-cleaning first and then the action of the hand was explained. The knack was the action of the thumbs working independently down the teat, which had to be held firmly by the fingers. It was a difficult co-ordination to obtain at speed which had to be constant — learning made one's forearms ache intolerably but that wore off as one got better. I managed without a flick from the tail or having my bucket knocked over.

At the end of the August course, Win and I found it difficult to get a real job together. Farmers had been prepared to take one woman but not two. However, the agent allowed us to continue working on the college farm — no pay — until we could find a billet. Our names went to the Exeter labour exchange. We were called for interview in the middle of September and met a rather hard-looking working farmer and his motherly-looking wife. She asked if we were prepared to 'live in', as there was really nowhere else within reasonable distance other than one of their men's cottages and they didn't think that suitable. She said we would be sharing a large bedsit and we could discuss the charge for it when we came to wage talk. We found this very encouraging — they had evidently decided to try us.

Mr D then said we would be general farm-labourers. His men had not been too happy about having women mucking in with them, but they were a fair lot and he wasn't expecting trouble, but we'd got to work and work hard — no lazing about or half doing

or out we'd have to go. Our work was mostly carting and fieldwork and general odd jobs as needed. The normal hours were 5.30am – 4.30pm and included necessary weekend work in rota with the men. Lunch break was three-quarters of an hour, taken to suit work in hand: our lunch would be at the farm, not in the fields. Mrs D broke in and said she'd not liked the 5.30am time, it suited the farmhouse better if we started at 6.30am and did the hour in the evenings, to which the men had agreed.

The rate for a general farm labourer was 15s. a week, less 3d. insurance (Lloyd George's money) and usually there were some perks given like potatoes, milk and cider. Mrs D said she wanted 10s. a week each for our board; this included reasonable personal laundry. Win and I couldn't believe our luck — they seemed so thoughtful and sensible. We said we thought it all sounded splendid and if they took us on, we'd certainly do our best.

We were greeted by Mr D on Saturday with his very old rickety car at Lapford Station in mid-Devon. Bury Farm was about two miles away, quite on its own, on the hill on the opposite side of the valley to the village. The Bury was a low, oldish two-storey house, at the back of a large cobbled yard. It looked comfortable and homely — like its mistress, who welcomed us warmly and said she was sure we needed a nice cup of tea.

After the tea Mrs D took us up to the bedsit. It was a large room

on two levels, looking out onto the yard, with panelled walls and the floor warmly carpeted — wonderful luxury after the dormitory. It looked comfortably furnished as we took in the sitting room level and thanked our landlady. She left us to settle in and we turned our attention to the bedroom level — the higher one. There was only one very large bed, with a small hood and side curtains, a wonderful quilt, two feather pillows and a long bolster. We looked at each other; it had never occurred to us that we might be expected to share a bed — neither of us ever had, and we lifted back the quilt and found the bed nicely sheeted and blanketed. Come bedtime we decided sides and got in together. Before we could do anything, we had rolled into the middle together and we just could not sep-

Posed in August 1916 at the Seale-Hayne Agricultural College in Devon, the students on a four-week course in farm work for young women include Gwen Stenning (front row, fourth from right). Do any other readers recognise themselves in this group? Miss Stenning is also pictured later at Bury Farm, Lapford, with her horse Kitty and a farm-cart.

arate to get out, try as we might. Feather mattress of course; we should have known and been more careful.

We found we each had a horse and cart in our care and use — I had Kitty, Win had Charlie. They were in stalls next to one another and there were two horses beyond, used by two men for ploughing and heavier work. We watched them put the head-harness on and then with effort managed to put ours over our horses' heads, by luck I think, and then came the heavy saddle. I'm sure Kitty knew she had a novice and thought she'd play up. She blew herself out; I got the saddle planted onto her back and got hold of the strap and pulled as hard as I could. Kitty let out her 'blow out' and round went the saddle under her belly.

Early in October it was all hands in the barn: the thresher was coming to thresh the corn. Duties by the men were known. Win had to feed the machine — I was at the straw-receiving end — outside one of the large store places. The thresher was like a steamroller; it came slowly hissing and smoking and was adroitly backed with much care, at the right distance from me and the store place. Both side doors of the barn were left open and the openings were higher than the funnel of the engine, so the smoke went out well.

When everything had been checked, the man who had to feed Win hoisted up the sheaves with a long fork. Maister received and straightened it on its way to Win, who clutched it and put

in into a cavity somewhere in the body of the engine. I had expected something the same size as the one put in to arrive, but was very surprised to find I'd got to handle spiky straw bundles as large as myself — I could only just lift them. Things came to a halt and a consultation on what to do started. I offered to do the forking up, very tentatively, and after being looked at with disbelief, the man who'd always done it said, 'Let 'er have a go — trial like', and handed me the fork. I could manage it easily and he agreed to do the stacking. My arms and shoulders ached for days after, but I wasn't going to give in at the time.

In the evening, when we reached our room, we found a large white sheet on the floor by the washstand and can of hot water. 'Mistress' had told us it would be there and we should undress on it; we'd find our clothes full of dust particles and seed, and we should put on clean things.

Alternate Saturday evenings we went in the car to Mrs D's family at Crediton. Her mother had invited us to join this family custom. The parents were elderly but very young and active with it and wanted to know as much as we could tell about ourselves, fortunately cut short by other visitors' arrival. There were three stalwart sons and two daughters, our 'Mistress' making the third. We were welcomed into a large hall, arranged for dancing, with a piano, lots of comfortable chairs and a long buffet table at one side of the room. The daughters took it in turns to play the piano and soon, after drinks of cider, ale, and soft drinks, the dancing began — waltzing and polkas, the latter being very popular, ending in a gallop. I was seized by the stalwart brothers in turn (no 'may I have?') and waltzed around so strongly I remember being quite breathless and almost dazed. There was a break half way and the long table was attacked: sandwiches, iced confectionery, cream buns, pastries, and a large fruit cake that Mrs D had brought and the drinks. It was always a very jolly, robust, friendly evening which we thoroughly enjoyed.

□ Let us correct our errors.

In the Winter issue on p.108 we gave Alistair Kilburn's telephone number wrongly. He is, you will recall, the man who has set up a hide in the New Forest, for paying badger-watchers. The correct number is 0425 403412.

Reviewing a splendid book called *From Carnac to Callanish* on p.121 of the same issue, I gave the author as Aubrey Burle. Forget that final 'e'; the name is just *Burl*. And several fans tell us that it is not (this was on p.10) Linda Snell of 'The Archers' but *Lynda*; I should have guessed.

There are a couple of errors from recent explorations which I must put right. When I went to Clwyd (Christmas '93), I visited a National Trust stately home which I called 'Erdigg' (p.166); it should have been *Erddigg*. And on p.147 of the same issue, in the introduction to Jack Jennings's article, 'The trees of yearning',

we spoke of Colcaenog Forest; it should be *Clocaenog*.

In Berkshire, in our last issue, I said on p.164 that the Speenhamland magistrates made their famous recommendation linking parish poor-rates to the price of bread in 1895. It was, I hope, quite clear from the context that we did know this happened in *1795*.

And finally, back in the Autumn of last year, I wrote (p.9) about a few very pleasant days I had spent at a guest-house on the Isle of Arran. I called the house Glencoy Farm. It should have been *Glen Cloy*. However, Vicki and Mark Padfield, who run this admirable establishment, sent me a Christmas card, so I hope I'm forgiven.   □

THE NATIONAL TRUST – PROTECTING BRITAIN'S HERITAGE

The National Trust is the country's largest conservation charity. Founded in 1895 as The National Trust for Places of Historic Interest or Natural Beauty, the Trust now protects on behalf of the nation over 580,000 acres of land, over 535 miles of coastline, some 230 major historic buildings and gardens, 20,000 vernacular buildings, over 1,200 farm tenancies and almost 1,000 industrial monuments.

Such ownership, conservation and property management does not come cheap and the Trust relies heavily on its members and supporters for most of its income. Other activities such as self-catering holiday cottages and shops and tearooms at Trust properties also help generate funds to support the Trust's work.

COMPETITION . . . COMPETITION . . .

"The Countryman" has linked up with the National Trust to offer readers the opportunity to visit Trust properties free for a year. The first prize in our competition is two annual passes entitling the winner and a guest to a year's free admission to National Trust properties throughout England, Wales and Northern Ireland, as well as a special "National Trust Picnic Kit", comprising a National Trust tartan picnic rug, a walking stool and "The National Trust Book of Picnics". Twenty runners-up will win copies of "The

Picnic rug and stool, part of the first prize.

National Trust Countryside Handbook", the essential guide to the Trust's open space properties.

All you have to do is answer the four questions opposite and send your answers on a postcard, with your name and address, to "National Trust Competition", The Countryman, Sheep Street, Burford, Oxford OX18 4LH. Your entry must reach us by Saturday, April 30th.

These pages were supplied

The first correct answer drawn on May 3rd, 1994, will be winner of the first prize. The 20 runners-up prizes will be drawn in the same way.

The judge's decision is final and no correspondence will be entered into.

Golden Cap from Ridge Cliff, Dorset, acquired under the Enterprise Neptune Scheme.

1. What is the name of the National Trust's campaign to save the unspoilt parts of Britain's coastline?

   (a) Enterprise Neptune
   (b) Coastal Rescue Crusade
   (c) Save our Seashores

2. What is the approximate cost of restoring one yard of traditional dry stone walling?

   (a) £1 (b) £6 (c) £12

3. In what year will the National Trust celebrate its centenary?

   (a) 1995 (b) 2000 (c) 2005

4. What is currently the approximate annual cost of maintaining the properties in the Trust's care?

   (a) £1 million (b) £10 million (c) £100 million

Looking towards Petworth House, West Sussex, from the lake. The annual cost of maintaining properties in the Trust's care is at least £100 million.

by the National Trust

and

The Countryman

EXCLUSIVE OFFER TO COUNTRYMAN READERS

EXPERIENCE "THE COUNTRYMAN" COLLECTION

EMI Records and "The Countryman" have joined forces to produce a celebration of the British countryside.

A compilation featuring the poetry and music of various artistes extolling the virtues of our Green and Pleasant Land, "The Countryman" is an evocative double cassette tape featuring amongst a host of others, Fantasia on "Greensleeves" by Vaughan Williams, The Watermill by R. Bing, Home Thoughts from Abroad spoken by Peter Barkworth, a selection of Country Dances (including the Floral Dance!), Shakespeare, an English Country Garden and humorous extracts from Morecambe & Wise, Flanders & Swann and Kenneth Williams. Introduced and linked by Jeremy Nicholas, it is as interesting and as diverse a collection as "The Countryman" magazine presents to you every other month.

This offer is exclusive to Countryman readers until May 20th and is available at just £6.99 including p&p (considerably less than the retail price when the tape goes on general release in May). To take advantage of this unique offer, simply fill in the form below and send with your credit card details or cheque made payable to Link House Magazines, to: Countryman Tape Offer, 120-126 Lavender Avenue, Mitcham, Surrey CR4 3HP.

Please send me .... cassettes.

I enclose my cheque (made payable to Link House Magazines) in the sum of £.........................

Please debit my Access/Visa/Diners

Number .... Expiry Date ....

Mr/Mrs/Miss/Ms ....

Address ....

....

.... Postcode ....

Signature ....

Offer available only within the UK. Expires September 18th, 1994. Please allow 28 days for delivery.

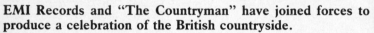

The Countryman explores

Dartmoor and South Devon

THE PONIES on the slopes of **Haytor Down** above are
a timeless **Dartmoor** scene — in more ways than one.
Haytor itself is at the very edge of the granite boss which

is the essential Dartmoor. The down slopes away eastward, into a mixture of softer rocks.

Nearly 300 million years ago molten magma, forming granite when it cooled, thrust upwards into the sediments above it. Above the intruding granite lay the Cornubian Mountains which were gradually worn away to expose the granite below. From the mountains the New Red Sandstone was carried down to the fields of Devon.

Later still — a mere 150 million or so years ago — a layer of chalk was deposited over Britain, and when it was eventually washed off the granite emerged to make the Dartmoor of today. Similar processes created the smaller south-western granite bosses of Bodmin Moor and the Isles of Scilly.

The wildness of Dartmoor is exaggerated in popular imagination because the contrast with the surrounding countryside of

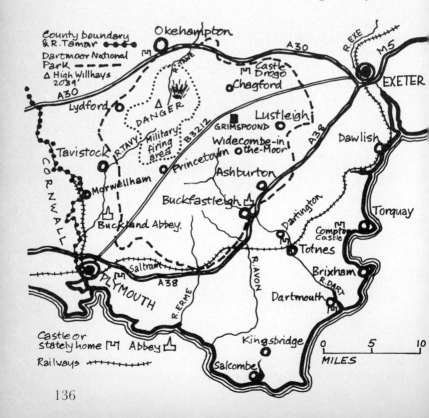

136

small fields, woods and stream valleys is so sharp. Sir Arthur Conan Doyle had good fictional reasons for hyping the wilderness when he wrote *The Hound of the Baskervilles* (1902), and Dr Watson's first view of Dartmoor from the train windows goes to the heart of it — *Over the green squares of the fields and the low curve of a wood there rose in the distance a grey, melancholy hill, with a strange jagged summit, dim and vague in the distance, like some fantastic landscape in a dream. . . . Rolling pasture lands curved upwards on either side of us, and old gabled houses peeped out from amid the thick green foliage, but behind the peaceful and sunlit countryside there rose ever, dark against the evening sky, the long, gloomy curve of the moor, broken by the jagged and sinister hills.*

Moor perils

Those who have made it their business to defend **Dartmoor** against many perils have adopted Conan Doyle's theme. 'The last wilderness of southern England' they have dubbed the moor — not accurately, for the prints of many centuries of man, from mesolithic to now, are all over it. But the inexactitude may be forgiven since the tag has served to save the moor from depredation as often as it has failed.

The moor is, of course, a national park and has been since 1951. It covers 365 square miles and contains the highest point in England south of the Pennines

(**High Willhays**, 2,039 feet). Despite the impression of loneliness given by the central moor, some 30,000 people live inside the national park.

Until the reforms of 1974, the national park was little more than an infrequently rebellious committee of Devon County Council. And the county council was only too willing to go along with the traditional attitude that since the moor was a barren wilderness it did not greatly matter what was done there. Long before national parks were thought of the first reservoir appeared — **Burrator**, built in 1898 and expanded 30 years later. It dams the **Meavy** and its offence is worsened by surrounding conifers. Today there are eight reservoirs on the moor.

The last to be opened (amid philistine municipal glee) was **Meldon** in 1972, which drowned the romantic valley of **West Okement** in the north-west corner of the park. In 1970 the Plymouth and South-West Devon Water Bill was thrown out by Parliament. It would have buried the **Foxtor Mires** where the little **River Swincombe** rises and flows to the **West Dart**. Instead the water engineers have gone to Roadford, off the moor and outside the park. This has meant flooding farmland — a cause of much bitterness among those to whom wild country does not appeal. On the other hand, the relatively deep valley is a much more economical way of storing water than the wide, shallow depression of the Swincombe.

Mass afforestation came to Dartmoor with the new Forestry Commission in the 1920s. The biggest chunks are around **Bellever, Fernworthy** and what is still labelled **Soussons Down** on the Ordnance Survey map, although the conifers removed any feeling of downland long ago. The fact that these belts of timber make cosy homes for siskins, crossbills and goldcrests is an inadequate exchange for the austere miles of moorland buried beneath them. But just as the reservoirs have ceased to be a threat, so has the march of the trees come to a halt. And Dartmoor still claims to be the only national park with more broadleaved than coniferous timber.

The most savage fight in recent years was over the route of the **Okehampton** bypass, the dual-carriageway extension of the A30 westwards around the northern flank of the national park. The choice was between a route within the park, south of the town, or across farmed countryside to the north. The Department of Transport wanted to go through the park, acting under strong pressure from the local MP, determined to save his farming constituents. The northern route had been on planners' maps for decades, and it certainly was a few millions more expensive (though but a drop in the ocean of road-building expenditure). After a public inquiry lasting nearly 100 days in 1979 and 1980, at which a certain Mr Michael Howard, who was then neither an MP nor a QC, spoke for the national park, the department decided for its own preferred southern route.

At this point the national park authority and the Countryside Commission gave up the struggle. Not so the Dartmoor Preservation Association — 'implacable but impecunious' as *The Countryman* called it at the time. The DPA demonstrated that the road would cross 'public open space' and therefore — the law required — suitable land must be given in exchange or Special Parliamentary Procedure must

Continued on page 144

Dartmoor is well signed, but the national park committee is not always as frisky in defence of the moor as it might be.

AUDREY HARBORD

Young Keble Martin on Dartmoor

Every summer, from 1904–1913, the three Martin brothers enjoyed a camping holiday on Dartmoor. The youngest, Keble (1877–1969), was an enthusiastic botanist and these expeditions laid the foundations for his famous book The Concise British Flora, *though it was not published until 1965. His elder brother Arthur (who became a church architect) kept the camp diary and illustrated it with these lively sketches. This article was first published in* The Countryman *21 years ago.*

ANYONE STANDING beside Petre's Cross on Dartmoor in July 1904, and looking north across the valley to Puper's Hill, would have seen the Martin brothers. One of their tents was home-made and the other — which could and often did sleep six — was an ex-army tent from Mr Tope of Plymouth. It had cost them 34s 6d. The three brothers camped regularly at the spot where the Warren stream met the Avon River (the Avon dam is a mile downstream now). Half a mile away then was the Warren House, and the warrener and his wife provided eggs and milk and an occasional rabbit pie. The brothers walked or cycled up from their home in Dartington Parsonage and reached the moor itself by Hayford Gate, often being joined by their Champernowne cousins from Dartington Hall itself.

Arthur Martin kept the day-by-day diary of camp. He also illustrated it, with his neat and informative architect's drawings, and showed every detail of camp life, including a sketch of a frog (sheltering, they said, from the rain) seated cosily inside his brother Jack's dog-collar on top of the grocery hamper.

Of the third and youngest brother, Arthur wrote, with a hint of exasperation, that he had 'suddenly informed the others in a distressed voice that his bed was made of *Tormentilla, Hylocomium squarrosum* and *Agrostis alba*. On further enquiry, they proved to be only a flower, a moss and a grass respectively'.

The young man with the botanical bed was Keble Martin and he would, in another half-century or so, become the best-selling author of *The Concise British Flora*. Already he was always being late, or temporarily lost on the moor, because of what Arthur lumped in the diary under the heading of 'Keble's botanising'.

Much of Keble's botanising was done in a wood below Sharp Tor, Harford, which came to be known as 'Keble's Wood' and may have been Pile's Copse. It was there he found a rare specimen of corydalis, or fumitory, and also a special fern, *Asplenium lanceolatum*.

1907 was an expensive year — they had to spend 10d on a teapot. And their list of 'suggestions for 1908' started off 'That the frying pan should not have any *large* holes in it', and more simply, 'That there should be a plum pudding'. One of Arthur's drawings that year shows the

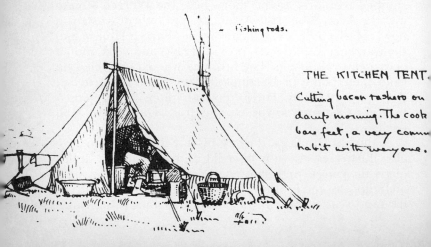

~ fishing rods.

THE KITCHEN TENT. Cutting bacon rashers on damp morning. The cook bare feet, a very common habit with everyone.

The Martin brothers' camp had two sleeping tents and a kitchen tent. Before the First World War, Dartmoor was almost uninhabited and there were no other holiday-makers to disturb the natural peace.

Jenny Quick kettle sitting on a new 'roarer' (methylated spirit, 2d, was another serious item in their accounts).

In fact they lived very well indeed. Most of the party were usually fishermen; Jack was a respectable shot and rabbit appeared often on the menu. But with the parsonage kitchens behind them, and the occasional hire of an ancient four-wheeler, they did not have to live off the land too seriously. The 'provisions consumed in Camp between July 25th and August 1st, 1909' included one leg of mutton (11lb), two beefsteak pies, one pigeon pie, 20lb bacon, 5lb plain cake and 12lb jam. Then there were the stores from Mr Tucker of Totnes, whose billhead proudly announced that he was 'Connected by Telephone — Number 4; Bacon and Hams Smoked on the Most Approved Method; and Maker of Totnes Butter Scotch'.

With two parsons usually in camp, Sunday was apt to be a busy day. On one occasion Keble set out at 7 am to

THE CHURCH

The brothers made a simple church beside their camp. Jack and Keble were both parsons and eventually Keble and Arthur designed and built a real church at Milber, Newton Abbot in Devon.

walk the eight miles to Dean Prior to take duty for the Revd Mr Perry Keene, who was 'toxophiliting in the Olympic Games'. Another Sunday saw Jack and Keble at the Warren House, christening the new baby. But the one permanent legacy from camp, which was held in ten consecutive summers, was the building of 'Church' in 1909. The entry for 4 July that year starts off with an account of Sunday morning on the moor:

> The morning broke dry and sunny. We did very little except mooch around looking for wheatears' or meadow pipits' nests, and watch various farmers and shepherds out after their stock. The latter seems to be the regular Sunday morning occupation, and each man was mounted and followed by a dog. Judging from the enormously protracted conversations held whenever two of them met, time was no consideration. We had Matins in a dell of rocks and ferns, on the way to the bathing pool. And it was on the spot we had just had Matins that we laid the foundations of Church. It consisted of a rough paving on the floor of the dell, then a flight of three solid granite steps with flanking boulders up to a small grass terrace and a granite pier with a cross on it, cut in the granite by Arthur with Jack's cold chisel and hammer.

The cold chisel did a good job. In 1949, Arthur's schoolboy grandson used his penknife to scrape away the lichen, and beneath it the cross was still firm and clear. The bathing-pool, which had been achieved during the camp years by widening and deepening the Warren stream (and from which, one year, they failed to rescue their only cake of soap), was also easily identifiable. But the Warren House had gone and was mourned, particularly by Arthur, who was now consultant architect to the Duchy of Cornwall and therefore knew most of the old buildings of Dartmoor, much of which is duchy property.

Arthur was also now a church architect of some standing, and he and Keble had another church under way, at Milber, Newton Abbot. In 1931 Keble had had a vivid dream in which he found himself taking a service in a church, shaped not like a cross but like a broad arrow. As he stood, in his dream, at the chancel steps, he could see the three aisles converging towards him. It was to Arthur, on the same day, that he sent a sketch of this unprecedented design, and on Arthur's London drawing-board the dream church of St. Luke, Milber, took shape. It was built, and in 1963 it was dedicated, with Keble himself present. One wonders if, on that occasion, his mind went back to the 'rough paving on the floor of the dell' where he had taken another service more than 50 years before, and where 'the early mornings were remarkable for the songs of the meadow pipits, which were soaring and parachuting all round Camp . . .'.

By 1913, when the last recorded camp was held, all three brothers had wives and families and the war was about to change all their lives. And there had been a population explosion on Dartmoor: for the first time the diary had recorded the sighting not only of birds and flowers but of two people. This was so remarkable that it got full coverage. The day had been spent watching a snipe's nest and exposing the nest of a wheatear which had built in a rabbit-hole. 'But the great excitement,' the diary went on, 'was the presence of a lady and gentleman who seemed to be having a picnic'.

How could they seem to have a picnic without actually having one? Perhaps they were illicit lovers. Or spies. Or just the very first tourists. □

143

Continued from page 138
be used, against which objectors have a right of appeal. Spending freely to gather and present its evidence, the DPA petitioned Parliament and persuaded the committee appointed to hear the matter that the road should not go through the park.

But the late Nicholas Ridley, who was then Secretary of State for Transport, was determined on the scarring of the park. He had the government's majority in the commons and its backwoodsmen in the lords whipped to overturn the committee decision. The road was built. The furzy slopes of the medieval Okehampton deer-park have been slashed by noise and **Bluebell Woods** have been desecrated. The woods were given to the people of Okehampton 'as an open space preserved for recreation and enjoyment by the public at all times' as a memorial to their daughter by the parents of the late Mary Ryan.

When Ridley died, Margaret Thatcher paid tribute to him as 'a great Englishman'. At Okehampton he was a great bully.

But for defenders of Dartmoor the running sore is the continued use of some 30,000 acres of land — nearly an eighth of the national park — by the Ministry of Defence. Helicopters clatter, red flags fly on skylines, roads have been bulldozed into the heart of the moor, artillery and automatic weapons are loosed off, cratering the peat and damaging ancient monuments — and, of course, the public is banned from this prime walking area, the highest land of the moor (see map on p. 136), on many scores of days a year.

It has long been the policy of the National Park to be rid of the military and to restore all this land to the peaceful uses which Parliament intended when the national park was set up, but the park seems to be weakening its resolve, perhaps because in 1991 Prince Charles, as owner of the Duchy of Cornwall, with extensive holdings on Dartmoor, renewed the army's licences for another 21 years. This was the longest extension ever granted and came at a time when changes looming in the defence world pointed towards reduced rather than expanded training needs.

The Countryman dropped in at the old Duchy Hotel (owned by the prince) in **Princetown** which is part of the park's spanking new High Moorland Visitor centre. Among all the displays and information there could be no doubt which was most popular with the schoolboys — a noisy, bang-bang, very professional video showing Royal Marines being trained on the moor. There was nothing here about the purposes of the national park. Watchers are taken through the training of commandos, right up to 'the proud moment' when they receive 'the coveted green commando beret . . . Now full of confidence, they appreciate the role that Dartmoor's wild and beautiful land-

Dartmoor's climate was warmer when Bronze Age man sited 24 huts in the circular enclosure of **Grimspound** *on the exposed northwest-facing* **Hameldown**, *1,500 feet above sea level in the middle of the second millenium BC. The people who lived here operated an elaborate system of reaves (boundaries) criss-crossing the moor.*

scape has played in ensuring the thoroughness and realism of their training,' intones the commentator in the style of British Movietone newsreel from 50 years ago. ' . . . As has been said by more than one newly graduated marine: "If you can survive on Dartmoor, you can survive anywhere".' (The film saves our blushes by omitting the standard squaddies' obscenity which doubtless prefixed Dartmoor in the marine's original words.)

None too subtly, we are reminded by the commentator that Dartmoor is an 'essential and *irreplaceable* training ground for professional soldiers' (our emphasis). Obviously the army plans no

withdrawal and must be highly chuffed to have found friendly houseroom on national park premises, where training for war can be promoted as one of the moor's normal, acceptable uses alongside peaceful farming, wildlife and recreation.

The park has, rightly, sought to extend its boundary in the south-west, where what one archaeologist called 'the complete ancient landscape' on **Shaugh Moor** is threatened. The stone circle and the associated field systems, which apparently began to be lived in around 1500BC, were granted a 30-year stay of execution in 1978 when it was proposed to bury them under the

145

overburden of adjacent china clay workings. Halfway to the deadline, the official review of the park boundaries has created a chance to bring the area within the park's protection. Unfortunately, the Countryside Commission, which ought to be backing such a move, has chickened out.

Perhaps the park's greatest achievement is the Dartmoor Commons Act of 1985 which set up proper management for its nearly 150 square miles of commons, about 40 per cent of the park's area. Not only has the act checked serious overgrazing by setting up a commoners' council to regulate farmers' activities, it also gave access on foot to all commons. The Ordnance Survey Outdoor Leisure Map now marks the huge areas of free access with bold purple lines. Dartmoor offers walkers the biggest tract of land in Britain where access is guaranteed by law.

In all these struggles to improve the park's opportunities for people to enjoy, to preserve its wildness and to prevent its desecration, a single outstanding figure has played a remarkable role. Sylvia Sayer, Lady Sayer by virtue of her marriage to the late Vice-Admiral Sir Guy Sayer, daughter of an established Dartmoor family, became chairman of the Dartmoor Preservation Association in the early 1950s and held the office through the two succeeding and crucial decades, and remained active in defence of the moor long after. In

the art of duffing up a council-committee chairman or minister with precision, economy and grace she has no equal. Sylvia Sayer celebrated her ninetieth birthday on 6 March this year; *The Countryman* and all who have been refreshed and inspired by her beloved moor salute her.

Church going

For those who appreciate ancient churches better than the late Philip Larkin did, this is a great countryside. Some of the interior riches are shown in George Hall's photographs of rood-screens (p. 54). In complete contrast are the austere profiles of the granite towers of the moorland churches. St. Pancras at **Widecombe in the Moor** (see p. 148) is in fact one of the more fanciful of them. W. G. Hoskins said it is best seen in winter against the moor rising behind. More than 30 years ago he warned that the village was terribly commercialised and he would surely weep for the place today. Here are the Shop on the Green, Widecombe Gifts, Cottage Gifts and the Tom Cobley Shop, but still in altered fashion the fair to which he went in the song on the second day of September.

On the other side of the moor **Peter Tavy** offers a bleaker profile, soaring above a village sufficiently off the beaten track not to have caught the tourist fever. In the churchyard monosyllabic family names on the gravestones reinforce the plain sim-

Transformation of the former **Tavistock** North station (above) from
public asset to private acres is complete, but freight trains still run as far
as **Meldon** quarry. Western region expresses thunder between **Exeter**
and **Plymouth**; the route includes fine scenic runs beside the **Exe** estuary
and **Dawlish** beach. From **Totnes** a seasonal branch ascends the
enchanting **Dart** valley. We may still cross the **Tavy** and the **Tamar**
on the exciting viaducts of a real, public railway from Plymouth to
Gunnislake. Its trains (one passes **Tamerton Foliot** below) survive
because the rivers hamper road access to the city from the north.

*The devil (it is said) came to **Widecombe in the Moor** to claim the soul of a man who napped during the service. He tied his horse a pinnacle of the church, which he then struck with a bolt of fire. The panicked horse tore down the pinnacle. This drawing is by Sylvia Sayer (see p. 146) who has defended Dartmoor against many devils.*

plicity — Mudge, Reep, Friend, Prout and Doige strike like blows of a bell calling across the moor.

Buckfastleigh — below the moor's southern edge — means **Buckfast Abbey** and half a million visitors a year. But before we descend to the great twentieth-century reconstruction of a medieval abbey beside the **Dart**, let us make another pilgrimage, to the Anglican parish church of the Holy Trinity on the hill above the abbey and town it serves.

Here is the tomb of Richard Cabell (died 1677), who was believed to be in league with the devil. Popular superstition was that his grave was haunted by great dogs breathing fire, and Conan Doyle may have adapted

the tale for his own purposes in *The Hound of the Baskervilles* — at any rate the tomb is a place of pilgrimage for aficionados of the great detective.

Was somebody up to devilish tricks in 1992 when a fire was started — deliberately it seems — near the altar of the church? It burned for some time in the small hours in its isolated position before anyone realised what was happening and called in the firemen. The church is now closed and the parish is wondering what to do with it. The Revd Paul Wilson, the vicar, told us that restoration to its former state would cost perhaps £5m — a sum far beyond local capacities. But the parochial church council is about

Like all Devon, this area is rich in nonconformist places of worship, the county having played a major role in the history of dissent. Right is the simple Bible Christian chapel at **Throwleigh**, dating from the early days of that missionary sect in 1839. Below is the elegantly emphatic Grecian Wesleyan chapel in **Ashburton**, fully expressive of the movement's self confidence at the same time.

to consider a scheme whereby a chapel would be built within the existing church plan. This could be used for services, including weddings, and the shell of the church itself might become a place for open-air events such as miracle plays.

The cost of this might be a more affordable £9,000. (Anyone who would like to help can send money to Patrick Ellis, 1 Tithe Barn, Buckfast, Devon TQ11 0EH, treasurer of the appropriate funds.) Meanwhile, the bells of Holy Trinity, damaged but capable of repair, and said to be the oldest peal in Devon, are stored ecumenically in the abbey, whither let us now descend.

There is no whiff of decay or financial difficulty here. A flourishing shop has much to sell,

including Buckfast tonic wine and honey from the bees which Brother Adam (now in his 90s), the great international authority, has bred, nurtured and saved from disease since he came to Buckfast as an 11-year-old from south Germany. There is nothing strange about that because the Benedictine community here was founded in 1882 by French monks and German novices on the site of the great monastery which stood here from some time before the Conquest, becoming a Cistercian house in the twelfth century, and surviving to the Dissolution.

The building is by any standards astonishing, which does not necessarily mean appealing. The story of how it came to be done is romantic if not miraculous: Abbot Boniface Natter, the

Brother Adam, the apiarist, is **Buckfast Abbey**'s *most famous inhabitant.*

first head of the refounded community, made known his wish to rebuild, but was drowned in a shipwreck from which his successor Anscar Vonier (1875–1938) was saved to become the driving force behind the building work.

The monks used a local 'blue' limestone (but grey is more accurate) for the outside walls. This is dressed with the yellow-to-gold Ham stone from Dorset around windows and doors and on the turrets. According to the abbey guidebook, the style is 'Cistercian transitional Norman'. Whatever it is, it is medieval. There are few concessions to this century, although the 1967 Blessed Sacrament Chapel, housing Father Charles Norris's exciting mosaic window of exploding purples, reds and yellows, is one of them. Like the abbey's preparatory school across the way (a low, crisp design of the same period by Lionel Brett and Francis Pollen), it makes one wish that Abbot Anscar's piety had moved him in a more contemporary direction.

Down south

Exchanging the bleaknesses of Dartmoor for the cosy fields of South Devon is plus or minus according to your taste in landscape. Certainly the triangle of land, which has its base on the southern flank of Dartmoor and its apex thrusting into the Channel at **Prawle Point**, is no place for a grand stride. The fields are small and the public-path net-

Blue Betsy seems a cosy local name for the periwinkle in this wild south-western part of Britain, but perhaps Betsy was a witch. Vinca minor *creeps, not through seeding but by rooting, in woods and on shady banks; it was introduced here in Roman times for its use in binding wounds and stemming bleeding — and also as an aphrodisiac. Sacred to Venus, it was highly recommended in the fourteenth century, if powdered with earthworms, as a way of bringing back the roses to married hearts: 'a rare quality' if true, remarked a sceptical Culpeper several centuries later. Medieval criminals on the way to execution were garlanded with* parvence, *the Old French name for the flower. Today's scientists value it in the treatment of diabetes.* **Engraving and words by June Crisfield Chapman.**

151

work is bitty. Off-road walking tends to be brief, followed by longish stretches on high-banked lanes which are alluring enough but are also busy and dangerous with traffic, especially in summer. Opportunities for walking are missing, too, in the most obvious and beautiful places — the valleys of the little rivers; few of these can be walked for more than half a mile or so at a time. Exceptionally, the **Avon** between **Loddiswell** and **Topsham Bridge** has a couple of miles of continuous riverside footpath. You can travel between **Buckfastleigh** and **Totnes** by steam train, hugging the **Dart** all the way, but not on foot.

The great walks are on the coast. The whole length of it carries the South Devon section (about 110 miles) of the national trail which rims the entire southwestern peninsula. It is, of course, a magnificent coast, but it has its bad moments — the conglomeration around **Torquay** and many appalling caravan sites. Typical of these blots is the clutch of some 40 immobile mobile homes, painted in an unfortunate pale green which blends with nothing, at **South Sands, Salcombe**. (John Piper always used to say that to disguise a horror in the countryside it should be painted black!)

But immediately above South Sands we enter National Trust land (its **Bolt Head** property), of which there is a blessed amount on this coast. The *cognoscenti* rate the mouth of the **Erme** (generally held to be the western boundary of the district known as the South Hams) as the best preserved in South Devon. It has no bridge or ferry. Walkers on the coastal path have to wade across at low tide between **Wonwell** (don't sound the second w) and **Mothecombe**. There is a period of some two hours during which, in good weather, this may safely be done.

The Mildmay family, long the landowners here, are generally credited with having resisted all the development that ruined other estuaries. The Mildmays' home at **Flete**, several miles up the Erme beyond the village of **Holbeton**, was originally a Tudor house. A prosperous late Victorian Mildmay called in the architect Norman Shaw to give it the works. The result is a romantic mishmash, for Mildmay could not apparently trust Shaw with freedom and parts of the Tudor original survive. The whole house was converted to appartments in the 1960s.

Torn towns

The Countryman stayed at the Marine in **Salcombe** ('very comfortable' as *Michelin* correctly avers), the sort of hotel where in mid-January you can bed-and-breakfast for a couple of nights for £70 with a decentish-dinner thrown in and have a balcony overlooking the water. Informal gentlemen must tolerate being questioned on arrival as to whether they have a tie in their baggage, and the cocktail conversation in the bar is about the rival merits of golf-courses (in South Carolina).

The town tumbles irregularly down the cliff to the estuary — a series of small streets and alleys running off the main street to the water. One of these takes you to the ferry for **East Portlemouth** (pedestrians only); otherwise cars rule here. A one-way system may have improved traffic-flow but it has made streetside life very unpleasant in just the kind of town where people should be able to stroll on the sidewalk and greet friends and neighbours in peace.

Kingsbridge's surrender to traffic has been just as dire. A long (quarter of a mile?) and utterly depressing car park occupies a splendid site (once that of the tide-mill and mill-pond) beside the upper estuary. The town proper is on the hill above and Fore Street survives as a bustling artery of some charm. It is dominated by the characterful clock on the town hall-cum-cinema. The slate-hung frontages are good and for the most part have not been expanded beyond their medieval proportions. There are at least three bookshops (new, reduced and second-hand) which must be a sign of an intellectually vigorous community and, with a bit of probing, there are some pleasant Georgian houses in need of a clean-up and vigorous dissenting chapels. The church looks

*The one-time village of **Hallsands**, at the southern end of **Start Bay**, is the sea's victim.*

down behind the main street, past more car parks, to an unfortunate industrial estate of the usual plastic beside the stream below.

Here is a town on a site to conjure with and with a still present sense of the past to relish; both deserve better treatment than they have had.

Similar themes repeat themselves in **Totnes**, the capital of the **South Hams**, and architecturally an outstandingly important town. Perambulate it with Pevsner in hand — a first-class educational experience. But traffic dominates, riding the pavements too often and, at the bot-

The Countryman explores

tom of the hill requiring a far too dominant road. This is made even worse by the truly dreadful supermarket (Safeway is the guilty party), which appears to consist entirely of restless triangles and mock beams.

In the upper part of the town it is a common belief of the shopkeepers that the waterfront developers are in league with the conservationists to remove vehicles from old Totnes and turn it into an Elizabethan theme park — a fate worse than traffic indeed.

Pony people

There are macabre names on this upper reach of the **Tavy** under Standon Down. There is **Coffin Wood** on the other side of the river and we are skirting **Chilly Wood** to find **Hillbridge Farm**, home to Mrs Dee Ivey and Marion Saunders, the latter being the chief but by no means only rescuer of ponies in distress on Dartmoor. The farm is a cheerful spot, with an untidy, cosy sitting-room with horsy books and cartoons along the walls. Dee is a diminutive lady with silver hair, who used to run the farm as a riding school. Marion is a cheerful blonde with a touch of the moor in her cheeks.

Visitors to Dartmoor suppose that the ponies they see in groups on the hills are creatures of nature; but if you were to get close enough to look (and we don't advise you try), you would find a pattern of nicks on the ponies' ears, each pattern denoting the farmer to whom it belongs. But ponies grazing wild more or less all the year round have problems. Dartmoor is locally said to have nine months winter and three months bad weather; after a long winter the animals are often run down and Marion's busiest time is in the spring before the animals have begun to recruit their strength, and before the grazing has recovered.

News of a stricken pony is not as simple as it sounds. To begin with, where is it? People who don't know the moor are vague when reporting an animal in distress. Few give grid references. Marion cannot risk calling out the nearest farmer to the area indicated. On the wide expanses of the Dartmoor commons, the animal could belong to any one of a long list of owners. So she sets off to find it in her moor-worn Land-Rover, supplied by the Horses and Ponies Protection Association for which she works part-time. She is its only employee with a specific rescue beat.

Once the pony has been found, things are easier than they used to be. A few years ago she would have had to Land-Rover back to a house or a phone-box. Now she has the mobile phone. The farmer can be called up and, if need be, the vet.

Hillbridge is home to a bunch of rescued ponies which are lovingly looked after. But neither Dee nor Marion, nor the voluntary rescuers from the Dartmoor Livestock Protection Society (which covers sheep and cattle also), can afford to be sentimental about the animals. Ponies were originally kept on the moor as work-horses, on farms or in mines. Now their value is what the farmer can get for them; most are sold at one of the three markets around the moor — **Tavistock, Ashburton** and **Chagford** — after the autumn drifts and selec-

tion. The likelihood is that they will finish up in a pet-food can.

'If they have had a healthy, free life on the moor,' says Marion, 'they have done better than a lot of animals.' What worries her much more are cramped pens at the markets and long lorry-hauls across Britain afterwards to the ponies' final destination.

Into the dark

'"Maybe thee be afeared?" said the working miner, "and if so be thee bee'st, thee'd better bide."' These words were addressed to the mighty civil servant, Mr Fidus Neverbend, on the occasion of his investigative descent into Wheal Mary Jane in Trollope's

*Marion Saunders (left) and Dee Ivey socialise with two of their contented ponies rescued from Dartmoor, at **Hillbridge** on the upper **Tavy**.*

novel, *The Three Clerks* (1858). Neverbend was already unmanned by descending three levels in buckets (*kibbles* was the miners' word), and now he had to go deeper still by 'a perpendicular iron ladder fixed firmly against the upright side of a shaft'. Trollope knew the South-West well, from the time he spent reorganising the postal services there, and had visited Devon Great Consolidated — then the world's richest mine — producing copper four miles west of **Tavistock**.

The mine's port was at **Morwellham**, four miles down the **Tamar**, and this is the place to go to rediscover the vanished industry. Today the Morwellham and Tamar Valley Trust is grad-

ually bringing the complex of port, mine, inclined plane, cottages, pub, water-wheel, lime kilns, etc. back to intelligibility.

We rode the narrow-gauge train of trucks into the hillside behind driver Colin West. Under his hard hat, a craggy profile suggests he might be a retired miner himself, but he turns out to be a keen *Countryman* reader, who was apprenticed to the printing craft in London and came eventually to have his own business. When the craft he had learned died, he came to Devon and took a summer job driving the train. A few years later, the trust asked him to make it permanent.

Colin describes the lives of men (lucky if they saw 40) work-

157

Stulls *in the main lode of Devon Great Consols copper-mine at* **Blanchdown**, *near* **Tavistock**. Stulls *were platforms giving cramped access to the* stopes *(working faces). The poet Coventry Patmore probably had this mine in mind when he wrote (1853) of 'swarthy tribes . . . Who, in hard rocks with harder wills, Pursued the crooked lode . . .'.*

ing underground in appallingly hazardous conditions for very low wages. He mentions the girls and women who sifted rock on the surface. He makes you glad to get back to the fresh air, which must be a tribute to his narrative skills.

Gentle fringe

Trollope knew about mines but said the prettiest scenery in England was 'on the southern and south-eastern skirts of Dartmoor, where the rivers **Dart**, and **Avon**, and **Teign** form themselves, and where the broken moor is half-cultivated, and the wild-looking upland fields are half-moor. . . . Men and women talk to me on the matter, who have travelled down the line of railway from Exeter to Plymouth, who have

spent a fortnight in Torquay, and perhaps made an excursion from Tavistock to the convict prison on Dartmoor. But who knows the glories of Chagford? Who has walked through the parish of Manaton? Who is conversant with Lustleigh Cleeves and Withycombe in the moor? Who has explored Holne Chase?' (Spellings are Trollope's.)

He is probably right. The fringe of the moor is a marvellous mixture of lush and lonely. In the end it won even the metropolitan heart of the poet Robert Herrick, who had the living at **Dean Prior** for some 30 years (interrupted by the Commonwealth). Or perhaps it was the local girls who charmed him ('If nine times you your Bride-groom kisse;/The tenth you know the Parsons is./Pay then your Tythe; . . .'). After the kisses he is buried in the churchyard, his grave unmarked.

Disconcertingly, there rise from this countryside two examples of architecture made in our time, at **Dartington** and **Drewsteignton**.

Dartington is the scene of a famous and continuing venture in the economic and intellectual revival of the countryside, launched in the 1920s by Leonard and Dorothy Elmhirst who used the latter's great wealth on the decayed 850-acre estate. Around the nucleus of the Great Hall are now buildings purely of the twentieth century.

Perhaps the most successful of them is High Cross House, built for the headmaster of the 'progressive' school which was one of Dartington's most famous endeavours. White, geometric and austere, it gloriously punctuates its Devon lane. Equally exciting is the contrast between Henry Moore's voluptuous but pinheaded 'Reclining woman' and the manicured yew-trees known as the Twelve Apostles to which she looks. And here is a theatre in which Walter Gropius had a hand and farm cottages by Louis de Soissons, a principal architect of Welwyn Garden City.

In one of the less successful modern buildings, Foxhole, we found John Elford, managing director and sole employee of Green Books, that gallant ecological publishing exercise. It is just the sort of concern which should find a home and feel at home at Dartington. Satish Kumar, who joined the wandering brotherhood of Jain monks when he was nine, founded the firm; now he has come to Dartington to direct Schumacher College which occupies the Old Parsonage just down the road, in the spirit of the man for whom it is named.

The stolid Devon countryside no doubt continues to wonder what 'all those beards and sandals' at Dartington are up to. A lot of the time they are up to hard economics like cider or glassmaking, timber production and farming. The beauty of the place is that they can also throw their hats over the moon and find space and opportunity for Green Books and Satish, whom many will think whacky, but who may be a true prophet.

On either side of Drewsteignton village, two castles rise above the woods of the Teign valley. To the east is **Prestonbury Castle**, an Iron Age fort; to the west **Castle Drogo**, which Sir Edwin Lutyens designed for Julius Drewe. He could afford to build a castle and have the top architect because he founded the Home and Colonial Stores (where are they now?). Lutyens would have preferred to build a decent country house, but his client wanted a granite castle. Although Drewe bought his spectacular site in 1910 and the foundation stone was laid the following year, the castle was not complete at his death in 1930.

The saddest room in the castle is the shrine to Drewe's son

Adrian, who was killed in 1917. But the whole building (well displayed by the National Trust) is a sad commentary on a failure of taste and money to match. Dartington has done better with the same ingredients.

Thank-yous

Our photographers were K. A. Coldman, p. 135; Christopher Hall, pp. 138 and 157; Leonard and Marjorie Gayton, p. 145; Mac Hawkins, p. 147; Christopher Stell, p. 149; J. L. Davies, p. 153 and R. H. Bird, p. 158. Stuart Seager drew the map.

We depended utterly on four Ordnance Survey Landranger maps (nos. 191, 192, 201 and 202) and *Devon* in the Buildings of England series (i.e. Nikolaus Pevsner in the edition of 1989, revised by Bridget Cherry). That book is dedicated to W. G. Hoskins and his *Devon*, in the 'new Survey of England' series (which never got beyond a few volumes), though published 40 years ago, is packed with leads and insights. *Nonconformist Chapels and Meeting-houses in South-West England* by Christopher Stell (published a couple of years ago for the Royal Commission on the Historical Monuments of England) was invaluable in this dissenting country. And we hope that we made good use of *Dartmoor, a new study* which, though more than 20 years old, has the imprimatur of Crispin Gill, who edited it just before coming to edit *The Countryman*. □

To make sure you receive a regular copy of
The Countryman, hand this to your newsagent.

☐ Please save me a copy of *The Countryman*

☐ Please deliver to me a copy of
The Countryman

ADVERTISING RATES

INCLUDING VAT

Lineage: **£1.06 per word (minimum 15 words)**

Bordered: **£29.38 per single column centimetre
(minimum 3cms)**

Box Number **£7.05**

**Advertisements should be prepaid, cheques made
payable to The Countryman and sent to Alison Jago,
Advertisement Manager, The Countryman, Sheep
Street, Burford, Oxfordshire OX18 4LH. Tel: 0993-
822000/823602. Fax: 0993-822703.**

**Alternatively, call Alison or Christine on 0993 822000
to read your advertisement over the telephone and
charge to your credit card.**

Please Note:
**Advertisements for inclusion in the Summer edition
published 20 May should reach us by 7 April.**

The Countryman's

MARKETPLACE

Where to find Crafts, Gifts, Books, Gardening, Plants & Tools, Holidays and Ideas

**To advertise call
Alison Jago or Christine Knight
on 0993 823602/822000**

Classified Advertisement
ORDER FORM

Please insert the advertisement below in the Spring/Summer/High Summer/Autumn/Christmas/Winter edition of The Countryman (delete as appropriate), until cancelled

Section ....

Credit Card No. [ ][ ][ ][ ][ ][ ][ ][ ][ ][ ][ ][ ][ ][ ][ ][ ]

Expiry Date ....

My cheque for £ .... is enclosed

Signature ....

Name ....

Address ....

....

Tel No ....

Address of cardholder if different ....

....

ROOM WITH A VIEW

Afloat

Hotels and Guest Houses

Hotels and Guest Houses

DEVON

THE GREAT TREE HOTEL
Nr Chagford, Devon TQ13 8JS
Tel: 0647 432491 · Fax: 0647 432562

R.A.C. 3 Star

A quiet and secluded old hunting lodge set in eighteen acres of its own gardens and woodlands on the edge of Dartmoor.

Delicious food, a cosy bar and a lovely relaxed atmosphere. A wonderful place to unwind and enjoy nature.

Special off-season rates June-August and November-March.

Fishing and riding available.

HEREFORD

THE HAVEN COUNTRY GUEST HOUSE
Hardwicke, Hay-on-Wye, Hereford HR3 5TA
Tel: 0497 831254

Early Victorian vicarage mentioned in Kilvert's diary, set in mature grounds with kitchen garden. Superb walking country crammed with castles, fascinating churches; 2.5 miles from the bookshops of Hay-on-Wye. Reputed for warm hospitality and excellent home cooking. Landscape painting course in September. Relaxing bedrooms (en suite or private bathrooms) with TV from £20 B&B. Disabled guests welcome in ground floor room.

NORFOLK

ASHWELLTHORPE HALL HOTEL
Near Wymondham, Norfolk NR16 1EX
050841 324; Fax: 050841 8409

An Elizabethan moated manor house, this family hotel is ideal for people with disabilities. Steeped in history and set in 15 acres of secluded, wooded grounds, the hotel makes an excellent base for exploring the beauties of the Norfolk countryside. Weekend and midweek breaks are available, plus speciality weekends, e.g. history, bridge, gourmet and fishing. Our superb English cooking features fresh local produce, mostly from our own gardens. Full licence held. Well behaved pets and children welcomed!

YORKSHIRE

LASKILL FARM
Hawnby, Nr Helmsley, York YO6 5BN
Tel: (04396) 268

ETB 🏵🏵🏵

Relax in our lovingly cared for stone farmhouse with secluded walled garden and lake. In the heart of Herriot country, the farm has 600 acres for sheep and beef cattle. Excellent cuisine is offered using home grown produce where possible. Packed lunch on request. Ground floor bedrooms, cot, high chair. Walkers' paradise with places of historic interest close by. Pony trekking locally. Eight bedrooms (5 en suite). From £16.50 B&B. Also 4 quality self-catering cottages from £180.00 per week.

Holidays with a Difference

THE LAKE DISTRICT
HIGHAM HALL
*The Lake District's
Residential Study Centre*

Everything at Higham has the stamp
of quality. Tuition, often provided in
conjunction with Newcastle
University, beautiful
accommodation, good food and idyllic
situation overlooking Bassenthwaite
with view of Skiddaw.

*"A unique country house experience at
a sensible price"*

For a prospectus and more
information phone 07687 76276
or write mentioning
The Countryman to:
Higham Hall, Bassenthwaite Lake,
Cockermouth, Cumbria CA13

HIGHLAND MINI-CRUISES. Explore
the Great Glen and Caledonian Canal
aboard 105ft Dutch Hotelboat.
Luxurious en suite accommodation, full
board, exclusive minibus tours. 3/6-day
cruises. Tel or write: *Bridge House,
Aberchalder, INVERGARRY,
INVERNESS-SHIRE, PH35 4HN.*
08093-428

EXPLORE DORSET. Heritage and
walking holidays all year from our
comfortable, historic home. Small
friendly groups. Single people very
welcome. Brochure: Anne King, *Newton
Manor House, Herston, SWANAGE,
BH19 2PQ.* Tel: **0929-427222**

EXMOOR WILDLIFE walking or tour-
ing holidays. We meet you at the station
and take you off the beaten track. Small
friendly groups. Single people welcome.
Also 4 day 'Safari' breaks. Details from:
Moorland Rover, Moorland House, St
Peters Close, West Buckland, Barnstaple
EX32 0TX. Tel: **0598 760 523**

TERRY'S MOUNTAIN BIKE HIRE.
Ride in the unspoilt Shropshire countryside. Routes from Tel: Church Stretton
724334/723302

SERENDIPITY FRANCAISE Special
Holidays. Choose from over 50 activities
in the Dordogne. Visit chateaux and
prehistoric sites or search for the wild
orchid and then paint it. Tailor-made
holidays for groups of 4 or more people
with a common interest. Tel: Mrs Green
0222-761439

EXPLORE THE MAGNIFICENT
North Pennines and more with an expert
local guide. Holidays/weekends include
tours by car, comfortable accommodation, good food. FELLDALES TOURS,
Fellview, Westgate, Weardale, Co
Durham DL13 1JR. Tel **0388-517516**

Enjoy a relaxed holiday in beautiful
surroundings and improve your
spoken French. Participants are
taught in small groups by
experienced tutors alongside French
participants learning English.
Joint activities facilitate conversation
and cultural exchanges in a French
environment.

**Details from: University of York,
King's Manor, York YO1 2EP.
Tel: 0904 433905**

TAKE A BREAK WITH ACORN

Riding•Fishing•Shooting
Sailing•Windsurfing•Yachting
Ballooning•Flying•Gliding
Golf•Tennis•Snooker
Country Lovers Weekend•Wildlife
Car Rallying•Off-Road Driving
Multi Craft Weekends•Bridge
Cultural Tour•Heritage•Elgar
Cider & Wine Tasting
Learn to Swim•Learn to Drive
Luxury Steam Train Trips
Murder Mystery Weekends

Free brochure with over 100 activities
ACORN ACTIVITIES
7 East Street, Hereford HR1 4RY
Tel: 0432 357335

A LANDSCAPE OF DREAMS. Weave and Design Holidays in the west of Ireland. Purpose-built studio and sophisticated accommodation. Send for free brochure to: Allie Kay, Phoenix House Studio, Whitegate, Co Clare, Ireland. Tel: **353-61-927109**

CYCLING HOLIDAYS. Rural France and Spain. Quality bikes, luggage transported, friendly back-up. Easter onwards. Brochure **0267-221182**

BYWAYS AND TRAILS. Minibus touring or easy walking holidays in the unspoilt Welsh Marches (North Herefordshire, South Shropshire and Mid-Wales). Holidays inclusive of all travel, including meeting you from the station if required, and accommodation in excellent country guest house in acres of lovely gardens. Holidays are at a leisurely pace with a friendly and informal atmosphere. Brochure: By-Way Holidays, Honeysuckle Cottage, Yarpole, Herefordshire HR6 0BG. Tel: (0568) 780252

CANAL WALKS
A great way for walkers to see some of the "real" Britain. To enjoy the peace and tranquillity of a waterside walk. Where the going is easy. Away from the hustle and hassle. Travel through hidden quarters of towns and cities. And see some of the finest countryside in Britain.
For 1994 we offer a choice of 20 walks, from 22 to 145 miles, all with confirmed bed and breakfast accommodation, luggage transfer and detailed route notes.
Towpath Treks
For full brochure, ring: **0296 395566**

HIGHLAND STEAMBOAT HOLIDAY. Cruise the beautiful sea-lochs and canals of Scotland in original coal-fired Clyde puffer — good food — comfortable accommodation. Send large sae for brochure: Nick Walker, *The Change House, Crinan Ferry, LOCH-GILPHEAD, ARGYLL, PA31 8QH.* Tel: 054-65-232

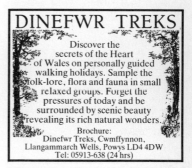

DINEFWR TREKS

Discover the secrets of the Heart of Wales on personally guided walking holidays. Sample the folk-lore, flora and fauna in small relaxed groups. Forget the pressures of today and be surrounded by scenic beauty revealing its rich natural wonders.
Brochure:
Dinefwr Treks, Cwmffynnon, Llangammarch Wells, Powys LD4 4DW
Tel: 05913-638 (24 hrs)

THE HOTEL, *ISLE OF COLONSAY, Argyll, PA61 7YP.* Map, full details (inc self catering) by return. Tel: 09512-316

QUANTOCK AND EXMOOR walking holidays. Small guided groups. Beautiful scenery. Please telephone **0984-56118** for our brochure

PERSONALISED HERITAGE TOURS. Southern England, chauffeured travel, country house accommodation. Huge choice: historic houses, gardens, churches, countryside, special interests. Church House, Shillingstone, Dorset DT1 0SL. Tel: **0258-860646**

Hotels and Guest Houses

AVON

SPRING BREAKS. Three nights B&B/ EM from £49. Bungalow in quiet hillside setting. Visit Cheddar, Bath, Bristol, Wells. En-suite available. Non-smoking. Brochure: **0761-462221**

BUCKINGHAMSHIRE

HEATHROW, quiet country cottage, 35 mins airport; b&b, parking, transport to airport. Tel: **0753-883724**

CAMBRIDGE

CAMBRIDGE, *St. Ives area.* B&B , EM optional, local produce, home cooking, WI member, disabled facilities. Tel: **0954-260359**

CHANNEL ISLANDS

GUERNSEY. Victorian guest house offering homely accommodation in St Peter Port and only 10 minutes walk from harbour. For brochure ring: **0481-713007/728847**

CHESHIRE

CUDDINGTON. Comfortable country cottage 12 miles Chester. Good walking country. B&B £15. Dinner available. ETB listed. Tel: **0606-882412**

CORNWALL

WEST CORNWALL. Convenient touring centre, residential area, friendly atmosphere, good food, comfortable accommodation. B&B, EM optional. Tel: **0209-718639**

CORNWALL. Mary and David Siderfin invite to your their home in sunny Cornwall — quiet residential district overlooking Falmouth Bay, and 10 minutes walk from town and beaches. Sae *4 Florence Place, FALMOUTH.* **0326-314108**

CARVEAN FARM, near *Truro.* Lovely secluded farmhouse, en suite rooms, log fires, antiques. Delicious home cooking, vegetarians welcome. Licensed. Stay one night or many. 10 mins A30, 15 mins beaches. Open all year. Tel: **0872 520242** for brochure

MULLION COVE 2 miles. Rural bungalow close beaches, coastal walks and golf. £12.50 pp B&B, HC, TV lounge. Tel: **0326-240492**

COTSWOLDS

BURFORD. Bed and breakfast in 14th Century Cotswold house in town centre. From £15. Private parking. No Smoking. ETB ♛♛ Tel: **0993-822418**

STRATFORD-UPON-AVON. Attractive Victorian house, quiet position — Old Town. 5 minutes walk theatre/town/ places of interest. Rooms have colour tv/ teamaking facilities, c/h. En suite available. Excellent English breakfast. Private car park. AA/RAC/Les Routiers recommended. Handy NEC — 35 minutes drive. Ideal touring base — Warwick Castle/Cotswolds/Worcester/ Oxford. **PARKFIELD,** 3 Broad Walk. Tel: **0789-293313**

'ARCHWAYS'. *LONG COMPTON.* Midway between Oxford/Stratford. ETB ♛♛ B&B, optional dinner in lovely 17th Century cottage. **0608-684358**

THE HILL, BURFORD. B&B from £15 in comfortable listed house. Town centre private parking. ETB listed. Tel: **0993-823843**

STRATFORD-ON-AVON, *COTS-WOLDS* 6 miles. Comfortable home, relaxing pool, vines. Dinner on request. Vegetarians, children, animals welcome. Three-night discount. Brochure: *Exhall Orchard, Ardens Grafton, ALCESTER, B50 4LB.* **0789-773032**

AMPNEY CRUCIS, *near Cirencester.* Delightful old converted stable block in its own walled garden, heated swimming pool, B&B and Dinner, excellent food standards. ETB ✷✷✷ HC AA QQQQ selected. Brochure on request: **0285-851-303**

BEAUTIFUL SOUTH COTSWOLDS. Picturesque Nailsworth. En-suite private bathrooms, 1 room suitable disabled. ½ hr Bath/Bourton-on-Water, 10 mins Westonbirt Arboretum. From £16 pp (10% discount 7 nights). Apple Orchard House. Brochure tel: **0453-832503**

CUMBRIA & THE LAKES

GRANGE OVER SANDS, *CUMBRIA, LA11 7HQ.* Clare House, delightfully situated in own grounds by the sea. ETB ✷✷✷ Commended. Open April to October. 4 day breaks in April £132.00; July/August and October £143.00. Please write for brochure or phone **05395-33026**

GRANGE-OVER-SANDS. *South Lakeland,* 'MAYFIELDS'. Charming small guest house, highly recommended for excellent food, home comforts and hospitality. Non smoking, private parking. Open all year. Tel: **05395-34730**

AMBLESIDE AREA — Ivy House, Hawkshead. Small family run hotel — sensibly priced. Tel: David or June Vaughan for brochure **05394-36204**

SOUTH CUMBRIA, *Arnside.* B&B private house for those who prefer home comforts. Tel: **0524-761778**

SILVERDALE, *South Lakeland.* Area of outstanding natural beauty. Equally outstanding guest house! Non-smoking. Fax/tel: **0524 701454**

DERBYSHIRE

PEAK DISTRICT. Georgian (Non Smoking) farmhouse, close to Chatsworth, Haddon and many NT properties. Be cosseted and cared for in our very comfortable home whilst enjoying imaginative (including vegetarian) cooking. Well behaved dogs welcome. *Matlock* Tel: **0629-583981**

EDGE OF PEAK DISTRICT. Family run rural guest house. Own restaurant, recommended RAC Good Food Route. B and B. Full or half board. Bargain weekends. En suite available. Two self-contained flats, sleeping 2/3 and 4/6. Phone *Dethick* **0629-534346**

DERBYSHIRE. Quiet accommodation offered at the part Elizabethan *Manor Farmhouse, Dethick, MATLOCK.* All rooms have hc, two en suite. Three Les Routiers awards. Ruth Groom, **0629-534246**

DEVON

DEVON / SOMERSET BORDERS. Comfortable farmhouse accommodation. Beautiful countryside. Ideal touring Exmoor/Quantocks/coasts. ETB ✷✷ B&B/EM £21.00 pp. Tel: Ann Heard, **03986-296**

FLUXTON FARM, *OTTERY ST MARY, DEVON.* Unwind in the peaceful seclusion of our 16th Century farmhouse, in the beautiful Otter Valley. Coast 4 miles. Pets welcome. Gardens, stream, trout fishing, comfort and superb food. **0404-812818**

171

HOLIDAYS

SOUTHERNMOST DEVON, Small Country Hotel magnificently situated in six acres of mature gardens overlooking the panorama of Slapton Ley Nature Reserve and Start Bay. Coastal and rural walks of outstanding natural beauty. All rooms overlook the sea. AA & RAC ★ Also four self-contained bungalows. *Greyhomes Hotel, Torcross, Near KINGSBRIDGE, S DEVON.* Tel: *Kingsbridge* **0548-580220**

See 'Countryman Explores' feature for more holiday ideas in Devon

---

SW DEVON, *Tavy Valley.* B&B in comfortable country house, originally part of mediaeval abbey. Lovely garden and idyllic setting. Friendly and informal. Tennis court. Tel: **0822-853285**

DORSET

BRIDPORT — *WEST BAY, WEST DORSET.* Britmead House. Renowned for hospitality, superb facilities and delicious meals. Ten minute walk to West Bay Harbour, Chesil Beach and Dorset Coastal Path. Full en suite bedrooms (1 ground floor) with TVs, hairdryers, etc. South facing lounge and dining room overlooking garden. Optional dinners, B&B from £18-£25. Open all year. RAC Acclaimed. ETB ♥♥♥ Commended. Tel **0308 422941**

BEAUTIFUL RURAL DORSET. Luxury B&B/EM. 18th Century thatched farmhouse, en suite bathrooms, sitting room, log fires, ch, super food. Tel: **0258-860646**

NEAR CRANBORNE. B&B rural bungalow, adjacent to Dorset Heavy Horse Centre. Pretty garden. Close to Cranborne Chase, within easy reach of New Forest/South Coast. Guest lounge, colour TV, every comfort. Tel: **0202-822954**

NEWLANDS HOUSE, CHARMOUTH, *DORSET*. Family run licensed country house. Close sea and NT estate. All bedrooms en suite, with ch, ctv and beverage facilities; smoking permitted in bar lounge only. Excellent food. Ample car parking. Single rooms and short breaks available. Write/telephone brochure: **0297-60212**

EXMOOR

EXMOOR. B&B in comfortable friendly XVII Century House. The Dell at Timberscombe for all seasons. Tel: **0643 841564**

ESSEX

ESSEX. Comfortable country B&B in Margaret Roding (AA/TB). Ideal short breaks, exploring, relaxation, etc. Tel: **0245-231509**

GLOUCESTERSHIRE

FOREST OF DEAN. Country house B&B, en-suite facilities, TV, interesting garden. Ideal walking/touring. Tel: **0594-832128**

NEAR ROSS-ON-WYE. Delightful country house, peaceful 5 acre gardens, oak beams, TV lounge, luxury bedrooms, delicious food, BB&EM, licensed. Special breaks. Anne Thompson, Tel: **0989-720417**

HEREFORDSHIRE

WYE VALLEY/FOREST OF DEAN. Comfortable guest house, set in rolling Herefordshire countryside. Cosy well appointed bedrooms and licensed lounges. Central for Ross-on-Wye, Monmouth and Hereford. And perfect for exploring river and forest, and the unspoilt Welsh Borders. B&B from £15. Tel: **0989-770 456**

HEREFORDSHIRE, *6 miles Kington.* B/B, delightful suite of rooms for two in peacefully situated Victorian house. Gardens, parking, etc. From £9. For details write: The Red House, Broxwood, Nr Leominster, HR6 9JH. Tel: **0544-340396**

LONDON

LONDON SW 1 — ELIZABETH HOTEL, *37 Eccleston Square, VICTORIA, London, SW1V 1PB.* Ideal, central, quiet location overlooking magnificent gardens on fringe of Belgravia. MODERATE PRICES. Egon Ronay/RAC. FREE COLOUR BROCHURE. Tel: **071-828-6812**

LINCOLNSHIRE

EAST LINCOLNSHIRE village, near wolds, fens and sea. B&B, tv, teamaking. Sorry no smoking. *Poundsworth, MAREHAM LE FEN, PE22 7QJ.* **0507-568-444**

NEW FOREST

BROCKENHURST. Bed and breakfast in 18th century cottage in village centre. From £15. Private parking, no smoking. Tel: **0590-22767**

NORFOLK

NORFOLK, *CLEY-NEXT-THE-SEA* 1 mile. *Flintstones Guest House, Wiveton, Holt.* Full ch, tea/coffee making facilities. Colour tv in all rooms, all en suite. Evening meal optional. Open nearly all year. Please ring to make bookings. Sorry no smoking. **0263-740337**

NORTH NORFOLK, *HOLT.* Elegant family-run Georgian hotel, ideal for bird reserves and coast. Beautiful views, excellent accommodation and food. Highly recommended. Bargain breaks. *The Lawns.* Tel: **0263-713390** for colour brochure

NORTHUMBERLAND

NORTHUMBERLAND / BORDERS. Peacefully situated country house, ideal base for Cheviot Hills, Holy Island and Farne Islands. Informal atmosphere, bed, breakfast and evening meal. Mrs Brown, *The Old Vicarage, Kirknewton, WOOLER, NORTHUMBERLAND.* Tel: **06686-219**

HERITAGE COAST. Cosy family run hotel in small hamlet. Bar/restaurant, all rooms en-suite. Also holiday cottages to let. *Cottage Inn, Dunstan, Craster.* Tel **0665-576-658**

NORTHUMBERLAND. Farmhouse accommodation on working farm, bed and breakfast, evening meal (optional). Quiet spot on A68 in National Park. Ideal touring centre. Sae: Mrs Evelyn Anderson, *Blakehope Farm, OTTER-BURN, NE19 1LQ.* Tel: **0830-520266**

OXFORDSHIRE

OXON/BERKS BORDER. Personal friendly service in comfortable home. Edge village in large grounds, own pool. Ideal walking country. Collection service available. Evening meal by arrangement. Tel: **0491-651548**

ISLES OF SCILLY

BEACHFIELD HOUSE. Derek and Mary Scofield welcome you to their comfortable family guest house, which is situated on the shore with unrivalled views. We offer a happy atmosphere with home cooking and a select wine list. Ideal for Spring and Autumn birdwatching. Send stamp for brochure to *Beachfield House, ST MARY'S.* Tel: **0720-22463**

COVEAN COTTAGE, *St Agnes, Isles of Scilly.* Perfect peace and tranquillity. Very comfortable accommodation, glorious sea-views. Excellent home-cooked meals. Personal attention assured. Tel: **0720 22620**

SCOTLAND

CHARMING, small, family run hotel standing in extensive grounds and surrounded by spectacular mountain scenery. Comfortable spacious rooms, a peaceful and relaxed atmosphere with a warm welcome and attentive service. Deliciously imaginative food. All bedrooms private facilities. Laundry room. Ideal for walking, birdwatching, golf. From £35 per person DB&B, attractive weekly rates available. Dogs welcome. STB ♔♔♔ Highly Commended. Yvonne and John Howes, Ardoch Lodge, Strathyre, Perthshire FK18 8NF. Telephone 0877 384666 for a brochure

NO CAR? NO PROBLEM! Be met at the station. Go on leisurely sightseeing tours of 'Bonnie Galloway', in our own 12-seater minibus (Wed/Wed holiday). For brochure: *Galloway Heritage Tours, Rosemount, Kippford, DALBEATTIE, DG5 4LN.* Tel: **055-662-214**

SPEY VALLEY. Country house in 6 acres. Excellent bird watching/walking. Good home cooking, all rooms en-suite. DBB £145 pw. Contact Maureen Taulbut, "Braes of Duthil", Carrbridge, Inverness-shire. Tel: **047-984 395.** STB Highly Commended. Non smoking

RIVERSIDE FARMHOUSE, b&b&em. Two twin rooms with en suite bathrooms. Home-made bread and farm produce. Trout fishing FHB. Prentice, Cockburn Mill, DUNS, BERWICKSHIRE. Tel: 0361-82811

HOLIDAYS

SCOTTISH BORDERS. B&B in comfortable country house, set in garden overlooking loch (SSSI) to beautiful Cheviot Hills. Evening meal locally. Mrs Hurst, *Lochside, Yetholm, KELSO, ROXBURGHSHIRE*. Tel: **0573-420-349**

EDINBURGH. *Rothesay Hotel, 8 Rothesay Place, EH3 7SL*. Central, 40 rooms with private bathroom, colour tv, tea/coffee facilities, telephone. Restaurant, cocktail bar, elevator. Reasonable terms all year. Tel: **031-225-4125**

INVERNESS. *EAST DENE GUEST HOUSE, 6 Ballifeary Road, IV3 6PJ.* Near Theatre and River Ness. Rooms with private bathrooms, colour TV, tea/coffee facilities. Brochure available. Tel: **0463-232976**

INVERNESS. B&B 10 minutes town centre. Panoramic views and peaceful surroundings. Warm, friendly service including complimentary pick-up from station or airport if required (1½ hours Heathrow). Tel: **0463-73768**

SHROPSHIRE

SHROPSHIRE B&B. Stay in historic Hall in heart of Welsh Marches near Ludlow (no pets). Mrs Watkins, *Broadward Hall, CLUNGUNFORD, CRAVEN ARMS, SY7 0QA*. Tel: **05474-357**

SHROPSHIRE. *Ironbridge area.* Farmhouse B&B from £12 in beautiful countryside. Trout and coarse pools. Lovely gardens and walks. Good home cooking. Ideal for Ironbridge, Telford, Shrewsbury, Chester. Melverley Farm, Rowton, TELFORD. Tel: **0952-770175.** CL site available. SAE for brochure

SOUTH SHROPSHIRE, LUDLOW. Country house luxury accommodation en-suite. Special offer: B&B 3 nights £45. All-weather tennis. Also s/c cottages. Tel: **058-473-296**

Nr SHREWSBURY. *Foxleigh House, Wem.* Two pretty twin rooms, private bathrooms, in elegant house on Shropshire Way. Ideal for touring, walking. ♥♥♥ Commended. Brochure: Mrs B Barnes, Tel: **0939-233528**

CHURCH STRETTON. Comfortable 12-roomed guest house (6 en suite) on lower slopes of Long Mynd. Two guest lounges, evening meals and packed lunches on request. ♥♥♥ ETB, RAC Acclaimed. Mrs Rita Rogers, *Belvedere, Burway Road, Church Stretton, SY6 6DP*. Tel: **0694-722232**

NEAR LUDLOW. Smallholding in beautiful south Shropshire hills offers warm, friendly welcome and DBB using own/local produce. No smoking. Brochure: John and Anne Coates, Fairview Green Lane, Onibury, Shropshire SY7 9BL. ETB WTB ♥♥ Highly Commended. Tel: **0584 77505**

NEAR LUDLOW. Grade II 17C farmhouse Welsh Marches village. Guests lounge, garden, CH, H/C. Splendid hill walking. B&B £15. Guided walks, navigation instruction by arrangement. Tel: **0568-86-647**

SOMERSET

QUIET CORNER FARM, *Henstridge, Somerset.* The name says it all. ♥♥ Commended B&B. From £16. Tel: **0963-63045**

SUFFOLK

SUFFOLK, CUCKOO FARM, *near HALESWORTH.* Quality accommodation recently restored, 1525, award winning farmhouse. En-suite, ch, log fires, B&B/EM optional. Non-smoking. Tel: **0986-82261**

HOLIDAYS

Hotels and Guest Houses

SUFFOLK, *near BURY ST EDMUNDS*. Delightful , quiet village setting. Excellent accommodation and cooking; B&B £16.50 single, £30 double. Tel: **0284-769340**

WOODBRIDGE. B&B. Town centre, secluded excellent accommodation, en suite, with all facilities. Own parking. Open all year. Non-smoking. **0394-383416**

SURREY

BOOKHAM COUNTRY HOUSE HOTEL set on the edge of Common Land. Within easy reach of several National Trust properties, Wisley Gardens and Box Hill. ETA ♨♨♨♨ Special weekend rates. For brochure telephone **0372-452742**

GATWICK B&B. Attractive Edwardian house, quiet location. En suite bathrooms. 12 mins airport. Parking facilities. Transport to and from Gatwick. Tel: **0737-248209** Fax: **0737-247663**

SUSSEX

BLACK MILL HOUSE, Aldwick, Nr Chichester, Pagham Harbours, Arundel Castle and Wildfowl Trust, Portsmouth Naval Heritage and South Downs Way. Family run hotel. Sea 300 yards. Enclosed garden. Lift, level access from car park. Short breaks all year. AA★★, ETB ♨♨♨ Commended. Tel: **0243-821945**

WALES

LLANDUDNO. B&B £12.50 pp. Washbasins, colour TV, tea/coffee making facilities all rooms. Close all amenities. Tel: **0492 871 322**

TINTERN. Excellent accommodation and a warm welcome at a small, 400-year-old guest house. Judith Russill, *Wye Barn, The Quay, TINTERN, Near CHEPSTOW, GWENT*. **0291-689456**

CONWAY VALLEY. *Glandwr, TREFRIW*. Personal service, home cooking. Dinner, bed and breakfast. Washbasins in all rooms. Cole, *Llanwrst 640431*

PEMBROKESHIRE. Warm welcome awaits you on a 220 acre dairy farm, centre of St Davids peninsula. Luxury accommodation, 10 en suite rooms. Children 10 years and over welcomed. WTB ♨♨♨ de luxe grade, B&B £20 per person per night. BBED from £28 per person, weekly rate from £185. Brochure from Mrs Jones, Lochmeyler, Pen-y-Cwm, Near Solva, Haverfordwest, SA62 6LL. Tel: **0348-837724.** Credit cards accepted

ANGLESEY. Georgian Country Guest House close to sandy bay of *Rhoscolyn*. Lovely coastal walks, ideal for bird watching and flowers. All bedrooms double glazed and en suite with colour tv and tea making facilities. Residential licence, home cooked meals. WTB Highly Commended. Brochure: **0407-860214**

SNOWDONIA. 17thC farmhouse at the foot of the *Moelwyns*. GR SH620421. Comfortable antiquity! Good food. Idyllic countryside. Walks for saunterers or dedicated ramblers. AA listed. B&B from £14. Dinner (optional) £9. *Bayley, Wern, Llanfrothen, Penrhydeudraeth LL48 6LX*. **0766 770556**

176

ISLE OF WIGHT

ISLE OF WIGHT. Needles coastline, small, very comfortable. ♛♛♛♛ AA hotel. Close to good beaches, downland walks. Any day bookings from £16.50. *Sandford Lodge, Totland.* Tel: **0983 753478**

WILTSHIRE

CONVENIENT to *BATH*. Recommended accommodation; B&B £12.50, em by arrangement. Mrs A Smith, *'Westbury', The Butts, Biddestone, CHIPPENHAM, WILTS, SN14 7DY.* Tel: **0249-713108**

YORKSHIRE

CLAPHAM, *YORKSHIRE DALES. Arbutus House.* Dinner, bed and breakfast. Central heating, open fires, home cooking, en suite facilities. Ideal touring, walking, relaxing. Telephone Cass family **Tel:05242-51240**

HELMSLEY, *NORTH YORKSHIRE.* En suite farmhouse accommodation with beautiful views, delicious food. ♛♛ Highly Commended. 2 nights db&b £66.00. Tel: **04396 221**

YORK. Top quality B&B £14 pp. TV, CH, hospitality tray. Close all amenities. Tel: **0904 659414**

COXWOLD, YORK. *School House.* Guest House and Tea Room. Homely accommodation in North York Moors National Park. B/B, Dinner by arrangement. CH, HC. Tv and drinks tray all rooms. Special weekly rates. J Richardson Tel: **0347-868-356**

NORTH YORKS MOORS NATIONAL PARK. Delightful holiday accommodation in charming old farmhouse. Secluded position idyllic surroundings. Ideal touring, walking, relaxing. Fine evening dinners and wines. Brochure: Manor House Farm, Ingleby Greenhow, Great Ayton, North Yorks TS9 6RB. Tel: **0642-722384**

YORK. *The Bentley.* Quiet, comfortable and within easy walking distance of city centre. Bedrooms furnished to high standards, some en suite. Parking. B&B £16 to £22.50. **0904-644313**

YORKSHIRE DALES, *GRASSINGTON.* Eileen and Allan invite you to share their idyllic 17C riverside cottage. Private fishing, parking. Home cooking. Friendly welcome. Winter bargain breaks. Brochure **0756-752463**

WENSLEYDALE. Stay in the Heart of the Dales at our farmhouse. Open all year. Panoramic views of Bishopdale. Lounge, open fire, licensed bar. Children, pets welcome. High standard B&B/DB&B. ETB ♛♛ approved. Pen View, Thoralby, Leyburn. Tel: **0969 663319**

DIRECTORY

Richard Jefferies Society. For information write to: Mrs S Povey, 20 Farleigh Crescent, Swindon, Wiltshire, SN3 1JY

Domestic Fowl Trust. Conservation of over 150 pure and rare breeds on display in breeding paddocks. Young stock available according to season. Full range of own design housing, equipment, books, advisory service. Large sae list. Open daily all year except Fridays 10.30-5pm. Honeybourne, Nr Evesham, Worcs WR11 5QJ. **0386-833083.** All stock guaranteed pure and healthy

Holidays Afloat

KENNETT AND AVON CRUISES aboard Bath's Hotelboat 'Harlequin'. Special interest cruises include: Industrial Heritage, Wine Tasting, Natural History. Details of our lovely holidays from: Sue West, Bath Hotel Boat Company, Tel: **0225 448846**

CANAL HOLIDAYS. Choice of 24 luxury narrow boats for weekly hire from central base. 2-8 berth all with central heating. Colour brochure from: **The Wyvern Shipping Co,** *Rothschild Road, Linslade, Leighton Buzzard, Beds.* Tel: **0525-372355**

OXFORDSHIRE NARROWBOATS. For a friendly peaceful holiday, cruise the beautiful rural Oxford Canal/Upper Thames. Top quality centrally heated 2-12 berth narrowboats. For a free brochure phone 0869 40348. Canal Wharf, Lower Heyford, Oxfordshire OX6 3PD

PICK A ROSE — Select fleet of 23 narrowboats based in leafy Warwickshire. Wide choice of routes. Colour brochure. Day, weekend or weekly hire. Rose Narrowboats Ltd, Stretton-under-Fosse, Rugby CV23 0PU. Tel: **0788-832449**

LUXURY CANAL NARROWBOATS. 2-8 berth. Many routes. Brochures from: **Simolda Ltd,** *Basin End, NANTWICH, CHESHIRE.* Tel: **0270-624075**

Holidays Further Afield

NORMANDY, HONFLEUR. Superb refurnished apt. overlooks old fishing port. Sleeps 4 from £160w. Tel: 0923-284418 anytime

PORTUGAL — RURAL ALGARVE. Villa with superb views in quiet, unspoilt area. Sleeps 2-6, own pool, maid. Sea 20 mins. Available for winter or summer sun. Tel: **0730-828205**

ANDALUSIAN FOOTHILLS, SOUTHERN SPAIN. Relaxing holidays with English couple in hilltop bungalaw with swimming pool. Airport collection, local trips, meals, drinks all included. For brochure tel: **(0403) 730661** (UK)

BEAUTIFUL CENTRAL FRANCE. Attractive cottage, sleeps 3/4. Walking country. Tel: **034282-2482**

All that is FRANCE, plus Auvergne Mountains, Nat P Park, old towns, spring flowers, cowbells. Stone Longere at 2,500 ft, comfortable, spotless, exclusively for non-smokers. Sleeps 4½. £220-£350 pw inc linen, etc. For details Di, in English, on 010 33717-86357 (odd tone)

NEW YORK CITY. Small bed and (home cooked) breakfast, countryish older home, fireplaces. Tramp nearby woods, then take historic ferry to Manhattan. Brochure: Hartshorne House, 88 Henderson Avenue, Staten Island, NY 10301 USA. Tel: **718-273-8105**

BEAUTIFUL newly remodelled cottage in the Poitou/Vendee/Charentes region of southwestern France. Sleeps 8-10 comfortably. (510) 842-5749 (USA) or (33) 46 26 36 60 (France) for bookings

FRANCE, *Southern Brittany*. Family cottage in splendid rural location. Villages nearby, coast about 12 miles. Sleeps 6. Well furnished with good facilities. Excellent for walking, cycling, relaxing. Tel: **05983-300**

UNIQUE ACCOMMODATION IN CORFU TOWN. Self-contained serviced apartments. All the year round. Heated, moderate prices. In one of the loveliest period town houses on the island. Details: Christopher Lavranos, 5 Mustoxidi, Corfu 49100, Greece. Tel: **061-25653**

ALPINE FLOWERS. Ground floor flat sleeps 2/3 in pretty French market town. From £110 pw. Tel: **0258-472748**

FRANCE, LOT VALLÉE. Our well furnished village house, with orchard, sleeps 4. Walking, tennis, swimming, restaurants, birds, flowers. Details: Tel **0233-840267**

PROVENCE, CAMARGUE. Farm cottage, also B&B. Rogers, Mas d'Auphan, Le Sambuc, 13200 Arles, France. Tel: **(01033) 90972041 Fax: 90972087**

FRANCE, DORDOGNE. Shabby chateau, lovely views and walks. Swimming pool, B&B, evening meal optional en famille. Tel: **0795 539551** or **010 3353 583518**

Self Catering Holidays

CAMBRIDGESHIRE

NEAR ELY. Ideal base for East Anglia. Cottage sleeps 4. Non-smokers only. £140 pw inc gas, electricity and linen. Available all year. Part weeks if required. Tel: **0353-860266** or write *31 Victoria Street, Littleport, ELY, CAMBS, CB6 1LU*

CORNWALL

RIVERSIDE COTTAGE: sleeps 4. Beauty and tranquillity. Ideal country-lovers and their dogs. Tel: **0579-50284**

HELFORD RIVER COTTAGE, *DURGAN*, sleeps 5/6, tv, ch. Close to beach and coastal walks, boats and sailboards nearby. *Falmouth* 0326-250119

CORNWALL, *Helford River*. Three charming properties at *Calamansac* in 30 acres woodland. Dinghy launching and mooring. Wood burning stoves, free wood, linen and CTV. Open all year. *Austen*. Tel: 0326-250339

CORNWALL. Charming waterside cottage *Nr Fowey*, ch & ctv, cove and cave at bottom of garden, dinghy available. *Polruan* 0726-870406

HOLIDAYS

CORNISH CRAFTSMEN'S COTTAGES

For your comfort and contentment, a small hamlet set around a private village green in heart of peaceful countryside, near sea. True luxury combined with old world charm. Generous heating, colour tv, linen, tennis, garages, and more. Also cosy 1-bedroom cottage, ideal for winter or summer holidays. All lovingly restored and cared for by **John and Nancy Jolliff, Tremaine Green, Looe, Cornwall. Tel: 0503-220333**

CORNWALL, *FOWEY HARBOUR.* Delightful individually-owned cottages, almost afloat or close waterfront, Polruan. Sleep 2/8. Superb views, exceptional facilities. Some properties have private moorings, accept dog. Available all year. Reductions for 2 people. Tel: **0726-870582**

SPECTACULAR NORTH CORNWALL, cosy cottage for two on peaceful farm close to Boscastle and coastal path. Two others with 2 & 3 bedrooms, open fire, central heating. Tel: *St Gennys* **(0840) 230470** for brochure

CORNWALL, *ZENNOR.* S/C luxury apartment, sleeps 4. Also chalet, sleeps 2. All around sea and cliffs. Parking. Tel: **0736-794117**

CORNWALL, *LELANT, near St Ives.* Cosy terraced cottage. Private garden, peaceful surroundings, close to Hayle Estuary. Sleeps 3-4. All amenities. Bradshaw, 13 Hellesvean Close, St Ives, TR26 2HQ for written details

ROSELAND. Modernised cottages, sleep 4. Ideal sailing, walking, birdwatching. Not June, August. Tel: *Portscatho* **0872-580706**

CORNWALL, *Polzeath.* 7 mins walk to superb beach. Heated bungalow, sleeping 4. From £120 weekly. Written details Tel: **0904-728604**

COTSWOLDS

BURFORD three miles. Quiet, comfortable cottage, sleeps three. Lovely views. Ideal for touring Cotswolds. Tel: **0993-823440**

COTSWOLD cottage, by stream, in quiet *BLOCKLEY.* Sleeps 4. Ch, open fires. Secluded garden. No pets. No children under 12. Tel: **0789-778674** or **0483-570323**

COTSWOLDS flat for two non-smokers. Peaceful garden, fine views. £90 pw including electricity. Also secluded caravan site. *Broadway* **853732**

OWLPEN MANOR, *ULEY, GLOS.* 9 special cottages in private wooded valley, sleeping 2-10. Short breaks. Dogs welcome. Tel: **0453-860261. ETB Commended**

MANOR COTTAGES. We offer personal service for quality cottages throughout Oxon/Glos. Linen and towels, colour TV, log fires. Airport collection and car hire available. Brochure: Village Farm, Little Barrington, Burford, Oxon OX18 4TE. Tel: **0451-844643.** Fax: **0451-844607**

CUMBRIA AND THE LAKES

CONISTON. Cottage overlooking lake, sleeps 4. No dogs. Tel: **05394-41461**

LAKE DISTRICT, *CONISTON* 2 miles. Converted cart-shed into comfortable, warm, self-catering on 16th Century hill farm. Peaceful countryside. Week or Winter weekends. Tel: **05394-41433**

COMFORTABLE CONVERTED BARN. Edge of Staveley village. Sleeps six. Non-smokers. Brochure: 0905 840631

Self-catering

HOLIDAYS

IDYLLIC LUXURY MEWS COTTAGES in Nature Reserve overlooking lake. Far from madding crowd but only 10 mins M6. Wonderful wooded walks next to RSPB Leighton Moss. *Challan Hall, Silverdale, LA5 0UH.* Tel: **0524-701054**

EXCELLENT SELECTION of self catering homes to suit all needs and requirements. Free brochure: Lowther Scott-Harden, 0768 64541 — 24 hours

LAKE DISTRICT village between *Ullswater* and *Haweswater*. Warm, comfortable 3 bedroomed cottage, sleeps 6. Modern kitchen, bathroom, full CH. Available all yar. From £126 pw. Tel: **081-670 6873**

GRASMERE. Comfortable well-equipped cottage, sleeps 4. With views over the lake. Tel: **05394-35209**

LAKE DISTRICT, ESKDALE. Comfortable, well-equipped cottage, sleeps 5-6. Wood fire, modern kitchen. Weekly until October; weekends or mid-week over winter. Brochure: Tel **09467-23340**

TWO'S COMPANY. Renovated rural cottage for two in South Lakeland, ideal base for walking, touring or sailing. No pets. Tel: evenings, *Windermere 46238*

LAKELAND, *BROUGHTON-IN-FURNESS.* Cosy cottage, sleeps 2/4. Ideal birdwatching, walking. Winter breaks available. Tel **081-459-2427**

HOWGILL FELLS. Three attractive, warm, well-equipped cottages. Superb views, large garden. Ideal for quiet, peaceful holidays. Easy access M6, Lakes/Dales. Two cottages with wheelchair access. Winter breaks a speciality. Brochure: Tel: **05396-23316**

DEVON

EAST DEVON. S/c annexe old mill. Beautiful valley, Blackdowns, 8 miles sea. Sleeps 4 (5). Linen & electricity included. Owner maintained. Tel: **0404-881497**

ATTRACTIVE 17C cottage, idyllic waterside setting. Also barn conversion, tranquil rural situation. Swimpool, tennis court, games room. For these and other quality character cottages in beautiful unspoilt area of Devon on/near coast Tel: *TOAD HALL COTTAGES* **0548-853089**

AXMINSTER 4 miles. Comfortable cottage, sleeps 2/4. Beautiful views, gardens, excellent base walking/sightseeing. C/heating, linen. Short breaks also available. Tel: **0460-220209**

MID-DEVON. ETB ⚑⚑⚑ commended cottage. Spacious, comfortable, well equipped for 5 + cot. Beautiful garden situation amidst farmland with wildlife. Central for Dartmoor, Exmoor, coasts, Devon Trust and RSPB reserves. Pets welcome. Brochure tel: **0363 84288**

See 'Countryman Explores' feature for more holiday ideas in Devon

HOLIDAYS

BETWEEN EXMOOR, BARN-STAPLE and Atlantic coast. Cottage for self-catering. Very quiet area. Ideal May/June walking. Tel: Hartnoll, **0598-710295**

CROYDE. Comfortable modern bungalow near beach. Super enclosed garden. Obedient pets welcome. Sleeps 5/6. Tel: **0271-890285**

NORTH DEVON, _CROYDE._ Comfortable bungalow near sea, sleeps six. Tel: **0594-529415**

BIDEFORD, _N DEVON._ Smallholding in remote tranquil setting has fully-equipped flat for 2 and a fully-equipped 6-berth static caravan. Paradise for country-lovers. Private fishing by arrangement. Bookings/enquiries: Mrs Williams **0409-241-285,** evenings only

---

DORSET

ABBOTSBURY. Peaceful, owner-maintained, self-catering coastguard cottage offers outstanding sea and country views. Excellent walking and fishing. Gardens with direct access to Coastal Path and Chesil Beach. Surrounded by hills, picturesque villages and farmland. Central heating, log fire, ctv. Tel: **0305-871746/871335**

'HEART OF DORSET.' A group of 20 self-catering cottages and B&B establishments throughout Dorset, all TB inspected. Brochure telephone: 0258 880248 or 0747 840666

BRIDPORT/WEST BAY. Spacious, modern, fully equipped bungalow. Sleeps 4/6. CH. Parking. Available ALL YEAR. From £116 pw all included. ETB ⚑ ⚑ ⚑ Commended. Tel 0308 422941

COMFORTABLE well equipped cottage near Shaftesbury. Quiet country location, sleeps 2/4. Tel: **0747-811103**

EXMOOR

EXMOOR. Cosy, secluded, cottage within friendly village. Overlooking countryside. Sleeps 2-4. £75-£140. Tel: _North Molton_ **05984-208**

EXMOOR PEACE AND TRAN-QUILLITY. Relax for a few days/week in countryside untouched by time. Marvellous walks — no noise — just quacking wild mallards on river beside s/catering, c/heated flats/cottage in NT village. Safe parking. Open all year. Brochure by return. The Pack Horse, Allerford, Nr Minehad, Somerset. Tel **0643 862475**

EXMOOR NATIONAL PARK. Very comfortable, well appointed holiday cottage in peaceful surroundings. Sleeps 3. No small children or dogs. Godsal, Edbrooke, Winsford, MINEHEAD, SOMERSET TA24 7AE. Tel: **064-385-239**

PORLOCK. Cottage, sleeps 2/3. Village centre, quiet location, close sea and moors. Tel: 0734-402650

EXMOOR _(2 miles Dulverton)._ Character barn conversion cottages offering outstanding accommodation in glorious tranquil setting overlooking the picturesque Barle Valley. ETB ⚑ ⚑ ⚑ ⚑ Highly Commended. Brochure: _DRAY-DON COTTAGES._ Tel: **0392-433524**

HAMPSHIRE

NEW FOREST HOUSE on forest edge, ½ mile from Brockenhurst centre. Sleeps 4. Ideal location. For leaflet phone **0272-735886**

HEREFORDSHIRE

HEREFORDSHIRE. Comfortable cottage in garden with lake, beautiful scenery, peaceful, colour tv. Tel: *Pembridge 388474*

BRADNOR HILL Farm Cottage, *KINGTON, HEREFORDSHIRE.* Panoramic views. Very comfortable. Well equipped. Sleeps 4/6. 100 yds golf and Offa's Dyke. **054-48-272**

IRELAND

NORTH CORK. Renovated farmhouse on private estate with idyllic gardens, woods, trout river. Sleeps 5/6. Ideal centre touring, walking, fishing, riding. Tel: **010-353-22-26145**

KENT

HYTHE. 18C cottage. Garden, garage. Near sea and North Downs Way. Sleeps 4-6. Tel: **0367-252842**

LINCOLNSHIRE

EDGE OF WOLDS. Secluded cottage in peaceful garden, sleeps 2. Tel: **0790 52477**

NORFOLK

WINDMILL and COTTAGES near Heritage Coast. Sleep 2 to 10. Brochure: **081-883-8137**

WEYBOURNE, *NORTH NORFOLK COAST.* Modern 2-bedroomed bungalow, in quiet location. Sleeps 4. Tel: **0773-716956**

NORFOLK, *SALTHOUSE.* Comfortable flint cottage. Equipped for owner, sleeps 4. Enclosed garden, view over Saltings, 10 mins beach. Tel: **0638-500385**

BRESSINGHAM. 18th Century cottage in peaceful countryside. Sleeps 4. Also B&B in farmhouse. Tel: Bressingham **(037988) 629**

SWAFFHAM 4M. Five delightful cottages in secluded, rural, 17thC barn. Sleeps 2-5. Children 11+, babies and pets welcome. Tel: **0366 328 794**

NORTH NORFOLK HOLIDAY HOMES,
Lee Warner Avenue, FAKENHAM, Norfolk NR21 8ER.
BROCHURE Ref. CM TEL: 0328 855322

NORTHAMPTONSHIRE

IDYLLIC SETTING. Superbly equipped country cottages. *Rye Hill Farm, East Haddon.* Beautiful gardens, historic houses, pretty stone and thatch villages. Ideal walkers, fishermen, birdwatchers, families. ETB ♦ ♦ ♦ ♦ Highly Commended. Brochure: **0604-770990**

NORTHUMBERLAND

NEAR BAMBURGH. Attractive cottage, own garden, pets welcome. Ideal for beaches, golf, birdwatching, walking. Tel: 0668-214283

HOLIDAYS

FULLY EQUIPPED centrally heated farm cottage. Views of Cheviot Hills, 5 miles Holy Island. Ideal centre, sleeps 5. Open all year. ETB 4 keys Commended. No pets/smoking. Brochure tel: 0289 88378

HOLY ISLAND, *NORTHUMBER-LAND*. Comfortable, modernised cottage, by sea, sleeps 6. Tel: **0483-472842**

VERY WELL EQUIPPED semi-detached cottage, sleeps 5, cot available, disabled facilities. On the edge of Northumberland National Park, near Scottish border, Kielder Water, Hadrians Wall. Ideal touring or walking. Tel: **0434-220250**

SCOTLAND

GALLOWAY COUNTRY ESTATE offers restful comfortable holiday cottages with salmon/trout fishing. Open all year. Sae Gavin Bain, *Munches, CASTLE DOUGLAS, DG7 1PD*

LOG CABINS and cottage set in extensive grounds with river and surrounded by spectacular mountain scenery. Comfortably furnished and fully equipped to a very high standard. Well heated. Laundry room. Ideal walking, birdwatching, golf. Pets welcome. Short breaks from £100. Weekly rates £180-£350. STB ✿✿✿ Highly Commended. Yvonne and John Howes, Ardoch Lodge, Strathyre, Perthshire FK18 8NF. Telephone 0877 384666 for a brochure

HISTORIC TAYSIDE. Well appointed farm bungalow. Two bedrooms and bathrooms. Near Blairgowrie, Meikleour. Ideal walking, touring, birdwatching (ospreys 3 miles). Golf, fishing, ski-ing, etc. Accommodation for horses. Available all year. Tel: Franki Bain, **0250-884 243**

BORDERS. Riverside s/c cottage, STB ✿✿, sleeps 5 + baby. Heating included. Ideal for children, trout fishing. FHB. Prentice, *Cockburn Mill, DUNS, BERWICKSHIRE*. Tel: **0361-82811**

ISLE OF MULL. Comfortable farmhouse, sleeps 4-6. Near Iona. Ferry, sandy beaches nearby. Birdwatchers' paradise. Also B&B available. Tel: 06817-260

NORTH FIFE. Self contained accommodation in converted cottage. Sleeps 2. Twelve miles NW St Andrews. Secluded rural situation. Tel: **082 624 217**

ABERNETHY FOREST, *STRATH-SPEY, CAIRNGORMS*. Comfortable cottage for 5 + cot. Peaceful woodland setting in mountain scenery. Scope for wildlife/bird-watching, hill walking, fishing, golf, riding, family cycling, touring. Brochure: Mrs Valery Dean, *Badanfhuarain, NETHYBRIDGE, INVERNESS-SHIRE*. **0479-821642** or **0381-620802**

ISLE OF MULL. Family stone cottage house, oil heating, superb doorstep coastal panoramic walking. Tel: **0223-352860**

ISLE OF ISLAY. Outstanding bird-watching. Warm, farm cottages, sleeps 2 and 5. G. & M. Jackson, *Coultorsay, BRUICHLADDICH, ISLAY, SCOTLAND, PA49 7UN*. Tel: **049-685-444**

MULL, near *Tobermory, Glen Houses, Dervaig*. Combine modern comfort and absolute tranquillity with superb views of the Bellart Estuary. Brochure tel: **0688-2111**

GRUINARD BAY, *WESTER Ross*. Spacious flat on working croft, sleeps six. Overlooking sandy beach and surrounded by spectacular mountain scenery. Also two 6-berth caravans to let. Tel: **0445-731-343**

FEARNAN, LOCH TAYSIDE, *Perthshire.* Comfortable, well-maintained cottage overlooking loch. Garden, access to shore. Accommodation for two. Central heating, TV, parking. Good touring centre, hillwalking, birdwatching. For full particulars Tel: **0887-830676**

SHROPSHIRE

SHROPSHIRE, *BISHOP'S CASTLE.* Stately home: spacious flat, splendid surroundings. Ideal children. 41 Cheval Place, London, SW7 1EW. Tel: **071-581 2782**

SOUTH SHROPSHIRE HILLS. Comfortable stone Granary with separate entrance and garden in secluded situation. Also self-contained Town Centre flat in historic *Ludlow.* Both well maintained, sleeping 4/5. Tel: **0584-75272**

SOUTH SHROPSHIRE. Exquisite 15th Century timbered cottage, set in glorious countryside between Ludlow and Tenbury Wells. Beautifully furnished, ch, colour tv, washing machine, etc. Sleeps 6. Pets and horses welcome. Tel: **0584-890-260**

COLEMERE, near Ellesmere. Peaceful location. Six self-catering country cottages for 2-6. All ETB ♟♟♟♟ Commended. CTV. Pets welcome. Brochure: **0691-623420**

CHURCH STRETTON. Comfortable cottage. Easy access (½ mile town centre), hill views, sleeps 4/5. Tel: **0694-723518**

SOMERSET

WARM PEACEFUL COMFORT. Holiday flat, barn conversion foot of Quantocks. Sleeps 4. Beautiful views, near coast, dogs welcome. Mrs Hill, Weacombe Gate, West Quantoxhead, Taunton. Tel: **0984-632773**

SUFFOLK

Near LAVENHAM. Delightful farmhouse flat, g/f, sleeps 4. Also, charming flat for 2. Gardens. No smokers. Over-60s reductions. Brochure: Tel: **0284-828428**

SOUTHWOLD, *Suffolk House* S/c flats, immaculate, full linen, colour tv, etc. Sea views. Sleep 2-4. Also pretty cottage and bungalow in charming village. All personally supervised. Available all year. Tel: *Southwold* **(0502) 723742**

SUFFOLK, *WESTLETON.* Delightful and well equipped accommodation in this charming village 3 miles from sea, with a garden and private parking. Sleeping 2/3. Owner maintained. Convenient for walking, golf, Aldeburgh Festival and Minsmere. Pets by arrangement. Tel: **072-873-520**

STONHAM ASPAL. Self catering cottages for two. Set amid 4 acres with pretty cottage garden. Tourist Board Highly Commended. For brochure contact Mrs P. Mead Tel: **0449-711229**

WALES

KITE COUNTRY. Dyfed near Dinas RSPB Reserves Rhandirmwyn. Beautifully converted stone barn. Also lovely converted cottage. Both fully equipped, each sleep 4-6. Landscaped garden, lovely countryside, excellent touring/ walking area. Gold mines nearby. Pets welcome. Tel: **0550-20188/21455**

IDYLLIC SECLUDED cottage (sleeps 2-4) near *Devil's Bridge*. Stunning scenery, walking, birdwatching. C/h. Dogs welcome. **0974-282631**

CAERYNWCH COTTAGES. Properties of a high standard in beautiful surroundings. Enquiries: Mrs P Richards, *Caerynwch, Brithdir, Nr DOLGELLAU, GWYNEDD, LL40 2RF.* Tel: **0341-422-263**

ST DAVIDS/SOLVA, *DYFED.* Comfortable stone cottage, village green, 2 miles sea, sleeps 7. Webster, **0296-748284**

ABERDOVERY. Cedarwood chalet, equipped for 4 persons (regret no dogs). Elevated position overlooking Dovey Estuary. Further details: **0432-274637**

RHAYADER/WYE VALLEY. Modernised stone cottage, sleeps 5/6. £80-£95 pw. Walking, fishing, trekking area. Tel: **093884-445**

NORTH WALES, *LLEYN PENINSULA,* 2 miles Aberdaron. Grid: 151258. Farmhouse superb quiet position overlooking sea. Sleeps 6. Sandy beaches nearby. Ideal walking, bird watching, fishing. Tel: **0628-522134**

PEMBROKESHIRE, *Near Manorbier.* Two bedroom holiday bungalow, sleeps 5. Quiet site 1 mile coastal path and beaches. Regret no pets. Tel: **0384-65282** evenings

N. WALES. Holiday camp chalet for six. Close Snowdon. Excellent base walking, climbing, golf. Tel: 0286-675963/4 quoting AM213

BORTH, *near ABERYSTWYTH.* Our detached house, garden, facing sandy beach, sleeps 9. Children, dogs welcome. **0970-871372**

ISLE OF WIGHT

For a peaceful holiday in the beautiful unspoilt West Wight. Two comfortable and well furnished self-contained apartments with secluded leafy garden overlooking bay. Ideal walking, sailing or relaxing on the beach. Short breaks and full weeks available. Tel: **0983-752216**

TOTLAND BAY. Luxury ground floor 2 bedroomed *apartment* overlooking Solent. Also well equipped 3 bedroomed *house.* Both near beach, beautiful walks. Non-smoking. Personally supervised. Winter Breaks speciality. Tel: **0983-755381**

YORKSHIRE

NORTH YORK MOORS and Coast, *Wydale.* Award-winning stone cottages in quiet, wooded, rural setting. Open all year. From £130 week. Brochure: **0723-859019**

IDYLLIC BECK-SIDE COTTAGE, *Stape, North Yorks Moors,* sleeps 4. From £130. Details: **0751-475477**

PICKERING. Gateway to North Yorkshire Moors. Character stone cottages set around secluded courtyard, superbly equipped, CH, grass paddock with play area, private parking, sleeps 4/5. ETB ♀ ♀ ♀ ♀ Highly Commended. Tel: **0751 473974**

Self-catering   # HOLIDAYS

ASKRIGG VILLAGE, _Wensleydale._ Three bedroom cottage with optional studio. Well equipped and maintained, col TV, CH, garden, parking, sleeps 6/8. Tel: **0332-780697**

YORKSHIRE DALES. Idyllic stone cottages and luxury holiday barns at _Settle_ and _Ingleton_, sleep 2-15, superbly equipped, babies/children/disabled/pets welcome. Tel for brochure, _YORKSHIRE PROPERTIES,_ **0729-840499**

REETH, SWALEDALE, _North Yorkshire._ Three idyllic cottages sleeping 2-7. Quiet location by riverside. Good walking/relaxing. All amenities. Details Tel: **0748-84273**

MISCELLANEOUS

ANTIQUES

BELLOWS repaired and renovated to their original usefulness, new pairs also made. Brochure from Wonnacott, Furzdale, Shebbear, North Devon EX21 5RB

BOOKS

FREE FRIENDLY BOOKSEARCH SERVICE. Mayhew Books, Great Chesterford, Saffron Walden, Essex CB1 1NZ. Tel: **0799 530649**

Almost Any Book Found. Free search, no obligation. Pickwick Books, Lavender Cottage, Shutlanger, Northamptonshire, NN12 7RR

Books Descriptive of the Traditional Rural Life of the British Isles. Rare and interesting out-of-print books on Rural Life and Traditions, Folklore, Rural Crafts, Gypsies, Windmills, etc. Wants lists welcome. Bi-monthly catalogues issued. Cottage Books, Gelsmoor, Coleorton, Leicestershire

Free List of Second-hand/Out-of-Print Crime Fiction Books available from R Andrews, 'The Barn', Brockhampton, Near Cheltenham, Glos

RURAL LIFE, customs and related topics. Rare and secondhand. Free catalogue. Country Books, Courtyard Cottage, Little Longstone, Derbyshire DE45 1NN. Tel/Fax: 0629-814223

BOOK-PLATES, personalised (21 for £2.99 + 30p postage) or plain (21 for £1.25 + 30p postage). Send SAE for samples to Editorial Services, 1 Piers Court Cottages, Stinchcombe, Dursley, Glos GL11 6AS (phone **0453-548888**

MISCELLANEOUS

H.P.Bookfinders. Established professional service, no obligation, no sae required. 6 Clerkenwell Cottages, Haddenham, Bucks HP17 8BJ. **0844 292083**

Unable to obtain a book you want? Free booksearch. No obligation. Sae for details. Find That Book (Dept CM), 74 Oxford Avenue, Guiseley, LS20 9BX. **0943-872699** evenings

Free Booksearch, any title found. Details to: Mrs M. B. Skellern, 1 Dobbin Close, Cropwell Bishop, Notts NG12 3GR. Tel: 0602 892068

Free Booksearch. Any book found. No obligation. No fee. Country Books, Courtyard Cottage, Little Longstone, Derbyshire DE45 1NN. Tel/Fax: 0629-814223

Out of Prints Books Supplied. Any title, old or modern. Contact Hooveys of Hastings for fast, no obligation service. Tel: 0424-753407. Fax: 0424-753407

Secondhand Books, all aspects English countryside. Write for list. English Country Books, PO Box 9, Moreton in Marsh, Glos GL56 0YU

LOOKING FOR A BOOK? Country/travel a speciality. Swithin Books, 42 Park Street, Wellington, Telford TF1 3AE

Authors invited to submit manuscripts all types (including poems) for book publication. Reasonable terms. Stockwell, Dept 377, Ilfracombe, Devon. **0271-862557** (Est 1898)

WANTED: ANY LITERATURE, PHOTOS, etc., on Belsize vehicles 1896 to 1925. Excellent prices paid. Turn out your attics PLEASE. Other makes considered but primary interest pre-1931. Box No 942, The Countryman, Burford, Oxon

CLOTHING & FOOTWEAR

Almost Unwearoutable Socks and Shooting Stockings, jerseys, fairisles, etc, knitted to order. Write for details: *Nicholl Knitwear, Corbridge, Northumberland, NE45 5PW. Tel:* **0434-632283**

Pure Cotton Nightgowns, kimonos and a range of simple ethnic clothes from India: shirts, skirts, waistcoats, trousers. Send sae for catalogue. *Denny Andrews (C), Clock House, Coleshill, Nr Swindon, SN6 7PT*

'Guernsey Gear' — Guernseys and zipper jackets by Le Tricoteur — NEW cotton Guernseys & wool V-necks. *'Specials'* for Ex-Tall and Ex-Large. LOW PRICES. Colour catalogue from: *'Guernsey Gear' (C), Uckfield, Sussex. Tel:* **0825-763764**

Handmade Ladies Viyella Blouses. Stamp for brochure and fabric samples. *Gillians, Dept CM, 14 Pinelands, Bishop's Stortford, Hedrts, CM23 2TE*

Dr Marten Shoes, Black, OxBlood, Waxy. Brochure: *Bernard Timson, 111 Hinckley Road, Earl Shilton, Leicester*

Knitting Wools. Shetland, Harris, Aran, Icelandic. Sae samples: *Achins Weavers, Lochinver, Sutherland, IV27 4LS*

Free Style Brochure & Cloth Samples! Hebden Cord Made-to-Measure POSTAL TAILORING SERVICE, famous over 70 years! Town and Country clothing tailor-made exactly as YOU want them. Country jackets, suits, trousers, plusses and breeches, etc, from quality traditional British cloths — Derby & Harris tweeds, Yorkshire worsteds, corduroys and moleskins. We guarantee an impeccable garment, at a sensible price. Special sizes are no problem. Send NOW for FREE STYLE BROCHURE with easy measuring instructions, and CLOTH SAMPLES (or your own material made up). Please state type of garment and material required. HEBDEN CORD CO LTD, Dept P8, Hebden Bridge, W Yorkshire, HX7 6EW. Tel: 0422-843152. Or visit us in the heart of the Pennines

COUNTRY CRAFTS

Traditional Bellows. Handcrafted in quality hardwoods in a range of styles to enhance your fireside. J Iliffe, 21 Elm Leigh, Frome, Somerset. Tel: 0373-466633

Appletons Crewel and Tapestry Wool By Post! Skeins 35p. Hanks £1.20p Shade Cards £10. Complete colour range. Postage included. *Lenham Needlecraft,* 13 Ham Lane, Lenham, Maidstone, Kent, ME17 2LL. 0622-858353

INTERESTED IN PATCHWORK? Ring 0273-515709 about patchwork pieces at bargain prices. £5 for starter pack

COURSES

WOODCARVING COURSES IN SOMERSET. Pleasant studio with comfortable accommodation nearby. Maximum five students. Beginners especially welcomed. Sae details: Zoë Gertner, *Deans Cottage, BAGLEY, WEDMORE.* **Tel: 0934-712679**

FOR SALE

NEWSPAPERS/MAGAZINES (1760s-1980s). Choose your date, ideal birthday present. From £15.95. Tel: **0492-531303** (9am-9pm)

GENEALOGY

Ancestry Researched: Devon, Dorset, Hampshire and Wiltshire. A Sutton, BA (Hons), 22 Gravel Hill, Wimborne, Dorset

Ancestry, Surnames, Coats of Arms expertly traced. J N Thompson, AGRA, St Ann's-in-the-Grove, Southowram, Halifax, HX3 9SZ

Scottish Ancestors need tracing? We can help. Write for brochure to: Caledonian Researchers, 7 Inverleith Place, Edinburgh, EH3 5QE

A Service created by experienced genealogists for those interested in finding their ancestors. Free details: Census Searches (B1), Lady Teviot, The Knoll, Stockcroft Road, Balcombe, West Sussex, RH17 6LG. 0444-811654

MISCELLANEOUS

GENERAL

Weather Instruments. Barometers, barographs, raingauges, hygrometers and thermometers. Also an inexpensive range of remote sensing instruments for wind, rain and temperature. All available by post. Full colour brochure and price list from Met-Check, Department GTC, PO Box 284, Bletchley, Milton Keynes, MK17 0QD. Telephone 029671-2354 (24 hours)

LEFT HANDED SCISSORS multi-use: dressmaking, hobby, household, tailors, nail, cuticle, pinking. Whites, 235 Seaside, Eastbourne, BN21 7NT

ACTIVE INVESTORS need looseleaf investment ledgers, £20. SAE for details to R. D. C. Passey, The Mill House, Crewe Green Road, Crewe CW1 1NW

NATURE

THE CLOUD WALL CHART 24″ x 18″. Twenty beautiful colour pictures of the cloud types with a description of each and what they portend. Cheques payable to M. Wickson (£5 inc p&p), Box 936, The Countryman, Burford, Oxon

PERSONAL

Person to Person - a friendly magazine for single people. Free details (Dept J.34), PO Box 4, Goring-on-Thames, RG8 9DN

Christian Singles. Social events. Friendship contacts. Houseparties. Holidays. CFF, Dept DT/B10, Edenthorpe, Doncaster

Psoriasis Sufferers, why not contact us for further information about psoriasis. Mrs Linda Henley, Department C, The Psoriasis Association, 7 Milton Street, Northampton, NN2 7JG

Rocking Horses. Realistic British Ponies, Unicorns, Gallopers or traditional Victorian/Georgian style wooden rocking horses. (Large and miniature versions.) Commissions. Restorations. UKIC members listed on Conservation Unit Register. Animal bedheads, furniture painting. BTG members. A.P.E.S. Tel: 074-579-365

Scout and Guide Badges and memorabilia wanted. Collections, books, etc. Contact Peter Berry, 21 Chard Road, Binley, Coventry

MISCELLANEOUS

Anybody Any Age Anywhere Able-bodied or Disabled. Choose your own ideal relationship. *Mutual Essential Links, 1 Weir Street, Northwich, Cheshire, CW9 5HL.* Tel: **0606 49093** (24hrs)

Oriental Carpets and Rugs purchased, sold, repaired, cleaned, restored. M & A Lewis, Wellington, Somerset. 0823-667430

AMERICAN PEN PALS. Selections based on your interests, age, etc. Satisfaction guaranteed! Free details: Transatlantic Penfriends, Box 2176-TC, San Pedro, California 90731, USA

KELLY KETTLE. Volcano water boiler is the ideal picnic companion because it kindles the comfort of a quality cuppa in the cold. Two pints of boiling water in only minutes with a sheet of newspaper and a handful of twigs. £35 inclusive. Stamp for details. KELLY KETTLE Co Ltd, Eydon, Daventry, Northants NN11 6PP

NATURAL FRIENDS. The nationwide contact magazine for single people of all ages who love the countryside, good health and the simpler things in life. Natural Friends (CM), 15 Benyon Gardens, Culford, Suffolk, IP28 6EA. Tel: **0284-728315**

PROPERTY

Private Purchaser requires substantial residential property in central London. Please send details to Box No 939, The Countryman, Burford, Oxon

Mill House or Period House with lake, stream, river, etc. 4/6 bedrooms, must be secluded. Oxon/Hants/Dorset/Wilts/Somerset/Glos. Must have minimum of 5 acres, although the more the merrier. Please write Box No 940, The Countryman, Burford, Oxon

Investment property with problems sought. Box No 938, The Countryman, Burford, Oxon

SOUTH COTSWOLDS (AONB). Former rural police house (3 beds) with adjoining police office, close to Badminton. Digital exchange for teleworking. Good motorway connections. Auction May 18th. Guide £60-70,000. Advance details Tel **0454-313305**

SPARE OR PROBLEM rural or urban land and buildings? Get practical ideas, advice and assistance on appropriate uses, development or reclamation. Moderate fees — staged payments arranged. For free brochure and initial meeting tel Landplan Consultancy, **0564 793476**

PUBLISHING

WANTED

CARS

Collector wishes to buy racing or sports cars (others considered). Please reply Box No 937, The Countryman, Burford, Oxon

VARIOUS

Watches, clocks, prints, Staffordshire, maps, very large books, pottery, lalique, oils. Please write to Box No 941, The Countryman, Burford, Oxon

The Countryman's Garden